Life's Scars and Wisdom

DEVANGEO HICKS

Copyright © 2020 by Devangeo Hicks

All rights reserved. No part of this publication may be reproduced, distributed, or transmitted in any form or by any means, including photocopying, recording, or other electronic or mechanical methods, without the prior written permission of the publisher, except in the case brief quotations embodied in critical reviews and other noncommercial uses permitted by copyright law.

ISBN: 978-1-953048-80-6 (Paperback)

The views expressed in this book are solely those of the author and do not necessarily reflect the views of the publisher, and the publisher hereby disclaims any responsibility for them.

Writers' Branding
1800-608-6550
www.writersbranding.com
orders@writersbranding.com

CONTENTS

Dedication v
1: A First Glimpse. 1
2: The Horrendous Death of Biological Parents. 4
3: Dealing with Early Childhood Teeth. 8
4: Kindergarten. 11
5: First Experience with Bullying. 14
6: The She Wolf. 20
7: Surviving High School. 31
8: Closing My Dreadful High School Life. 41
9: College Life Rolls Around. 45
10: The Rock of Our Family's Death 52
11: My Very First Job. 65
12: No More Grieving 70
13: Second-guessing College. 75
14: Picking Back Up Where I Left Off 81
15: Summer School and Field Placement 95
16: Fall Internship and Graduation 102

Dedication

This book is dedicated to both my grandparents Jessie Mae Glosson and Famon Hicks who's resting in heaven. They both played a big impact on my life growing up and they're part of the reason for this old soul that I have today. Both of y'all passing really hit me hard because I thought my life was over but little did, I know, it was only just beginning. Without the both of them, I wouldn't have the wisdom that I have today as a young man, so thank both of you for instilling in me that God is the answer to all things when I'm feeling down, and even when I'm feeling down, like I can't make it. He's always there to lend a helping hand. Thank you for the many memories and life lesson's that was bestowed upon our family. Rest easy, for everything I do now is for you.

*Pain and suffering has emerged the strongest souls;
The most massive and inferior characters are sealed with scars.*

—Devangeo Hicks

1

A First Glimpse

Ever feel like the weight of the world is on your shoulders and it's just too much to bear at one time? Like everything you've ever loved has been pulled from underneath you within an instant? I never knew what that feeling was like back then until a few years ago when it all hit me at once and unexpectedly. It was like a slap in the face that I had to pay attention to, had I not, I would've kept on learning the same lesson over and over again and that was just something that I was not willing to do since I'm getting older now. Sometimes we tend question God's work on things that we seem to have no control over, and we often ask ourselves within that moment, Why me of all people have to go through this process in my life that was not expected? I always found myself saying I wasn't prepared for this or nobody told me that this was gone happen. What did I do so wrong to deserve to be put in the predicament where I had to wipe the tears from my own eyes, stand up and face the world like a man while trying to carry the weight of the world on my shoulders?

I know we're not supposed to question what God takes us through in our everyday lives, which we may call an emotional roller coaster, and we don't know if it happens to better us as people or to hinder us and make us that of what you call handicapped. Being that I'm a lot older now, but still no very young, I'd say some of the things that happens are to help elevate us for the places that he is about to take us. Learning from my past experiences, of what I've been through over the past few years, I now know that God won't put more on us than we can handle.

As I sat back and thought to myself, it may have been that extra push I needed to grow up and go further in life, seeing as I was always known as this sheltered child that couldn't do what everyone else could do based on the kind of parenting that I had. I never understood any of that as a child, but now that I'm a little older, I must say that it has played a significant impact on how I live my day-to- day life and sometimes communicate with other people as well. I went from feeling like I had everything to being knocked down a few notches that put me in a situation where I really had to put my life into perspective and count the many blessings that I already had because somebody would always remind me of how good I had it, compared to some other people because it was somebody else out there going through worse than what I was going through and would trade places with me in a heartbeat. It's not like I was complaining about my life, I just didn't like the fact that I felt smothered from time to time. I couldn't explain the pain that I was going through because everything seemed to be a blur to me as to what my next move was gone actually be.

As I sat there so helplessly with the tears in my eyes starting to fall due the heartache I couldn't seem to take. The pain and misery I felt then and still feel until this very day is a feeling that still has me at a loss for words and a little shook up about difficult situations on how I live life when being put into difficult situations. I sometimes tend to overthink a lot of things that play out in my life. It's like I'll fold on any little task that's given to me because of the experience and confidence that I lacked. Some would say the feeling is indescribable. The Lord knows I wouldn't wish what I'm going through at the moment on anybody because it can affect my ability of being able to succeed and how you view things as they play out. The fear of not knowing what is coming next as you try to blend in and keep it all together from falling apart because that's what people want you to do or at least that's what they expect.

It came to a point that I didn't know who I was and nothing at that point seemed recognizable to me. I thought I was going crazy because I couldn't fully function in all the things that started to take place in my life so unexpectedly, especially after dealing with the loss of my grandmother a few years ago which really hit home not only for me, but my whole family because we all became divided and went our separate ways, which tore me to shreds on the inside emotionally that I all I had ever known. Trying to hide it and cover it up as if it wasn't there is what made it worse and made me felt like I was going crazy. I let a lot of it bottle up inside of me to the point that I had no choice but to try and fight it off because I didn't want that taking control of me anymore.

Even now, I can't even explain how it makes me feel, I just know I wouldn't wish this on my worst enemy, not that I have any that I know of. It's like this empty feeling of doubt and regrets that just eats at you and tries to pick at your flesh until there's nothing there left to pick at. Seeing how everything played out over the years, I can honestly say I know who's truly there for me and who just pretended to be there in the heat of the moment. With everything that I've battled and still battling till this day, I take it all with a grain of salt and keep on pushing because, at the end of the day, nobody's going to look out for me like those three family members that have remained constant in my life, even with our ups and downs that we went through. So I cope with how my cards have been dealt to me because I'm still at that age where I'm learning, and fuck ups are bound to happen in the midst of just that by itself. Lately, I've been learning how to deal with difficult people when it comes to certain situations in my everyday life, even when odds are stacked against me. I sometimes catch myself and say "that person is battling something more serious and go on about my day". Let me take you all from the beginning on how this all started and came to be what it is today in this current time.

2

The Horrendous Death of Biological Parents

I came into this world on April 22, 1994 to be exact. Now I grew up without my actual biological parents, not knowing who they were or what they even looked like or how they appeared because I was basically a newborn when this fiasco started to take place. I've just seen pictures of my mama lying around the house, and my grandma and grandpa telling me stories of who she was and how she used to be when she was here. They'd often tell me stories of what she was like and some of the things that she did, and from what they told me, she tended to be a bit of a handful or as some may actually say, a bit hotheaded. She and my so-called father didn't really get along to well the whole time that they were together, and at times, he often threatened to kill her whenever they got into serious conflicts that could've been overlooked and not that serious if you ask me.

Now, I think that could've been a sign from God himself that she needed to leave him alone then, especially when someone flat-out, constantly threatens to take your life the way that he did with her. It was also said that he'd physically abuse her a couple of times because she wouldn't do whatever he told her to do like he was a control freak that would watch her every move. I know that she was very young when all of this took place and he was a lot older, so that may have had something to do with it. From what I was told, he was a womanizer and just wanted her to be up and under him 24/7 without letting her breathe. It also sounded like he may have been a little insecure, so he did things like lash out at her all the time. One of my aunts said that she had to get physical with him a few times when he put his hands on her. After so many physical encounters that they seemed to keep having, they were then told to separate from each other because he kept threatening to kill her. After a while, he became more violent. The man was so crazy, my granddad had to give my mama a gun just to protect herself at all times, but that didn't stop my daddy from doing what he wanted to do, which was to keep tabs on my mama. Everyone knew he wasn't wrapped too tight in the head and knew he'd try something once they had split up being the type of person that he showed himself to be. It was even said that being in the military had kind of thrown him of his head mentally and that if he threatened to do something to you, he would most definitely try.

 After being separated for a while, he then got it into his head that my mama was supposedly seeing someone else since she stopped talking to him, which was true in the first place because she stayed on the move with someone else traveling all the time to the point of where you would never know where she'd actually be until she gives someone a phone call. He took it upon himself to go pay her a visit one night in the apartments and see what she was up to since they had to split up. We stayed in the apartments located in a small city. Living in the apartment were my mama, one of my older cousins and me. That night, my daddy made his appearance on the scene to go see what was going on because he was always like this private investigator, trying to see what my mama was up to all times when not in his presence. They said he had to have busted into the house because she had all of her doors locked so that he couldn't get in with her gun ready. After he broke the door, he and my mama started arguing back and forth sharing their words with a bunch of combativeness towards one another. My cousin was scared, so she went out to call for help because it's like she knew something was bound to happen with him making an appearance the way that he did after he was specifically told to stay away from her. From what I've heard, my daddy was crazy and was always going around, threatening people's lives whenever he got into a slight altercation especially when he was intoxicated with liquor. While my cousin had left to go get help, he then pulled his gun out and pointed it in her direction. His exact words before pulling the trigger of that gun and killing her were, "If I can't have you, nobody can". He then pulled the trigger with no remorse, firing the bullets directly into her chest, killing her and leaving a bloody body all over the floor. After he shot her, he then proceeded to pick her up and throw her body out the window and onto the ground. He went and got both my brother and I and sat us right next to one another, letting us know how much he loved us and the he would've done anything for us. My thing is, if he actually had love for us as his kids, he would've respected our mother who gave him his kids and let well enough be. Knowing the action he had committed, he didn't want to face life in prison for taking another person's life, or I guess deal with the fact of that being on his mind constantly receiving hate for what he did, he instantly picked up the gun again where he laid it and put it to his head. He then fires the gun again, blowing his own brains out onto the floor, scaring my brother and leaving blood splattered everywhere in the place.

    I wasn't old enough for the violence that took place to affect me. Therefore, the sound of the bullets when they fired in the house that night didn't have any effect on me. I guess the people next door heard a lot of what was going on and called the police immediately. By the time the police arrived, it was already too late because it was already done. Coming in after the police were my grandparents who were rushing to see what was going on. They look so devastated knowing that their daughter was already dead. I can't imagine what they felt at that moment because it all happened so fast and who would expect that the situation will get worst. Good thing that my dad was already dead by the time, my granddad could have shot him dead for killing his daughter. I knew it was a traumatic experienced for both of them.

    Till this day, I wondered what it would've been like had my mama done what my granddaddy had ask her to do and used that gun to defend herself when he came busting in the place like some crazy mad man. My mind often reverts to stuff like that, but I can't have any flashbacks because I wasn't even old enough to walk or talk when all that took place. Both my mama and daddy's funerals were held the same exact day and time in different locations. The people from my daddy's side of the family wanted to bury both him and my mama right beside one another. But as furious as my grandparents were with him about what he had done, they wanted nothing to do with him or the planning of his funeral, which I can't blame them for. I wouldn't want anything to do with the planning of his home-going celebration either because he was the one that cause of both theirs in the first place with his malicious antics. After the funeral was over and everything settled down, everyone mourned the loss of my mama, things started to lighten up a bit as everyone had to adjust to the fact that she was gone and no longer be with us anymore, left my grandparents to take both my brothers and I in and raise us up to become young men. That later went down the hill when I got a little older and everyone started noticing it, so that led to an even bigger problem. My grandmother had already a lot of experience raising children because of her own and some of my other cousins she had already raised while in the process, which were her grandkids as well, so that wasn't any big deal to her when it came for her to get custody over us.

3

Dealing with Early Childhood Teeth

As a few years began to pass us by and I got a little older, I found myself being quite active as a child with somewhat of a smart-mouth at a very early age in the way I was brought up. My grandparents would always to tell me how they would carry me around in a basket, and I'd sleep right at the foot of my grandma's bed in the little basket right next to her. My grandma developed an emotional attachment to me quickly, so she took me wherever she went throughout her day. It was just like she was a new mom all over again after all those years watching over two babies and a toddler, who was still like a baby himself. I had the closest of an attachment to her as well because, whenever I was with her, I felt warm, safe, and secure, believing that she would never leave my side no matter what the outcome was.

Growing up in a big family can have its ups and down, especially when you have a lot of roaming eyes watching how you get treated compared to them as children and they feel the need to be vocal about it. I'm not saying my grandparents showed favoritism or anything of that sort; it's just that some they was a bit more hard on one than others, and some of them saw that and I got the blame for being the way I was. I had always been curious as a child, especially around the ages of four and five. At that age range, I began to grow into who I was going to be and developed a little more personality to be who I wanted to be. My grandparents would bless me tremendously, with candy almost every single day, especially my grandfather. It was probably because he loved it so much himself, and every time he took a trip to the store, he would bring this specific kind back. He always ate his favorite candy, called Strawberry Dreams, which he would get from the dollar store right along with a soda water or two that he called it, to wash it down after eating an entire bag. It was his go-to every time he had a craving for sweets or he just wanted something to nibble on here and there. I ate so much candy with him back in the day, especially that candy in particular that all my teeth started to decay from top to bottom, causing me to have to go through specific surgery as a child to get all my teeth capped with silver little crowns so my teeth can grow back the right way.

Going into surgery, I remember my dentist telling my grandparents that I couldn't eat nothing after a certain time, considering the type of surgery that I was getting ready to have. I was scared that morning because, as a child, I didn't know what I was getting ready to go into being that I was so young and everything that came out of the dentist mouth sounded so scary for me to hear. It was the most painful surgery; all I remember was a bunch of dentists standing around me, going inside my mouth, capping each tooth that had decayed.

My teeth had to be in critical condition for them to have to cap every last one of them when we only thought that a few was getting capped. The doctors tried giving me some medicine to try and put me to sleep beforehand so that they could work on my mouth without me feeling a thing, but as scared as I was at the time, sleep was the furthest thing from my mind. When they saw that the medicine wasn't working, they came and got me from up front anyway and took me straight to the back where they soon began the process. They came in to work on my mouth, and all I could remember at the time I was kicking and screaming for dear life like they were killing me. I cried through the whole process of them capping my mouth with a bunch of silver crowns, which I thought was pretty dope when it was finished. Others didn't think so well of it because they weren't used to seeing something as such. I was in so much pain at the time. I could hardly eat anything and I mostly just slept on the way home. Everyone else didn't seem to like them as much as I did. They would pick on me as usual, which wasn't anything new to me. It even got to the point where I was teased by my family at times and by other kids my age for the longest until my adult teeth started to come in as the crowns fell off. My mouth bothered me for months until I got used to them, which didn't take too long for me to adjust to. All my teeth had caps on from front to back.

My self-esteem dropped drastically, and I would constantly talk down on myself for the way that they made me look because of how others looked at me whenever I went out in public with my grandparents. Other kids would stare and point at my mouth whenever I opened my lips to say something. Going through all of that as a child and hearing how everybody would already tease me and call me ugly, not considering my feelings, hurt and bruised me because it made me feel that nobody was considerate as to how I felt. Especially when I got into an argument with someone, they'd instantly crack a joke about how my teeth looked. I got picked on mainly by my family because I was around them 24/7, and they basically made it seem like I didn't have any teeth in my mouth at all or probably because they weren't white crowns that was put in my mouth instead. They even gave me a name back then where they called me, "bald-mouth catfish," which I never understood because I had teeth; all of them were just capped underneath.

After about a year had passed, my adult teeth slowly started to appear with the caps falling out of my mouth left and right like the doctor had mentioned throughout my checkups. So it was a good thing that they didn't last too long. Most of them had come back just before I even started school with the other kids, although I still had a few left in my mouth, but by then, most of my adult teeth had finally came in even though they grew kind of crooked.

4

Kindergarten

I was able to start school about three years later. I had always wondered why all the kids my age and those older were going to school while I had to stay at home every day with my grandparents up until the age of about 5. They told me it was because I wasn't potty-trained at around the ages of three and four, so that caused me to have to sit out of preschool both of those years, which caused me to be behind or be at a disadvantage when it came to learning compared to the other kids.

A year later, after I finally got potty-trained and I was able to go to the bathroom by myself. My grandma tried getting me into preschool, but there were no available slots, leaving me with no choice but to attend regular school and go straight to kindergarten. I had wanted to go to school with everybody else for the longest, but when it came time for me to go, that was a whole different story because all hell broke loose that morning I was getting ready. I was cool until I got on that bus and went straight to the school because I was so used to sitting at home and being with my grandparents that I didn't want to leave them at all by the attachment that I had to them.

Once I got to the school, I threw one of the biggest fits. I gave the teachers pure hell on the first day because I didn't want to be there with the rest of the kids, and I wasn't used to new faces or being in that kind of environment. I didn't some of the other kids because I had never seen them a day in my life, and I didn't care that my two cousins my age, whom I practically saw like every day, were in the same class as me. I just knew I didn't want to be there because I had never been in any place without my mama and daddy next to me. I yelled, kicked, and screamed until my mama (grandma) came back and got me because at first, it seemed like nobody was hearing me out because I was a child. I ran across that mean older lady that had this hairy mole on the side of her face, who tried to make me stay by saying, "He needs to be here with kids his age. Let him cry and throw a fit all he want. He will be just fine." The look on my face said it all once she said that, and just from hearing that, I screamed even louder to make them want to send me home.

After so many attempts and bribery that didn't seem to work, they came and got me and took me home because I wouldn't stop throwing one of the biggest tantrums there was. I thought I would never have to go back again once they came and got me until my mama sat me down and told me that I'm going to have to go to school unless I wanted her to go to jail. And she wasn't about to do that, so she made me go every single day even when I faked being sick. And some days when I really was sick, she'd still make me go, and I'd literally had to throw up in front of the class, just for them to come check me out, and that's only because she knew how much I hated going to school.

Eventually things started to change, and I got better, but that was the only way she got me on that bus every morning because, other than that, I wasn't having none of that. It was hard for her to let go, but she felt it was time for me to branch off from them and leave the nest to be with kids my age so that I could become more social and adapt to new things. We all know that one of the hardest times in a parent's life is knowing when to let go, and I struggled through that a lot as well just as much as she did with me, being that I was a sheltered child ever since the death of my biological mother and my grandparents being all that I really knew.

With that being my first year in school, I didn't excel like the other kids because I sat out during the time they were in preschool learning. So it was very difficult for me at the time to learn as quickly as they did. We would have a new book every week with that current alphabet on it in upper and lowercase letters we were learning. The other letters and words seems unfamiliar to me that made me difficult to understand. So there are lessons that are easy for me to understand

and sometimes difficult maybe because I started so late which made me so frustrated in the first place.

The school year went by with me hardly knowing anything about school and what it was for, I got behind and failed one of the easiest grades it was in the book and got teased and picked on for just that. Things were said to me such as, "how you fail that easy grade?" or "All you ever do is take naps." I had to repeat kindergarten with a whole new group of incoming kids who were a year younger than me, but only this time around. It didn't take long for me to adapt and interact with everybody because I already knew what to expect from being in school that current year before that. Now I'm not gone lie, school confused the hell out of me my first two years, but I eventually got the hang of things and went from there.

The next school year after that I finally went to the first grade, which was a big deal compared to kindergarten back then because the kids thought they were so much older. I caught up with one of my cousins, who had left me behind back in kindergarten two years before that, so I'm feeling like I was the man to make it to first grade. I was considered to be a baby when I was in kindergarten, or that's what the first graders would always label us since they were like only a step ahead of us.

5

First Experience with Bullying

I then encountered my first bully, who used to bully me by saying that he was going to lie and snitch on me if I didn't do what he tell me to do. Now at that time, I was considered a good student because I never really got into any trouble like the other kids did. My attitude changed drastically compared to when I first started. I thought then that the reason why I was being bullied because the bully didn't like the fact that I haven't been into trouble before and my teacher always brags on how I behave in class and how different I was from the other kids.

I believe that's what led him to want to pick on me in the first place, but I wouldn't necessarily say that he was picking on me, it was more like trying to call me a bluff. He wanted me to do whatever he said, which wasn't going to always happen because he tried to make me look like a fool while doing it. I did what he said sometimes, like a fool that I was, just to avoid unnecessary trouble and confrontation with any of the teachers just in case they believed him. It wasn't like I was scared of him or anything of that matter, but I somehow knew that it would've been my word against his and I didn't have time for any of that. I mean we were just only kids and didn't know any better at the time, so I played along with it because I didn't want anyone to think differently about me or my character. When I was young, I thought I was already wise compared to the other kids, I played the role very well just so he wouldn't snitch. It's like I was always trying to do what everyone else wanted me to do instead of putting myself first, and that played an effect on me so bad.

It's not something that I'm proud of now that I've gotten older and I now realize my faults in that I've taken a lot of crap from people as an innocent child just because of me being a nice person and even till now, I hate it when people take my kindness for weakness because, once I'm pushed to that point of not caring, it's no return of what you may get after. I think the guy was kind of jealous and maybe a little envious of me anyway and of how much special attention I received that he wanted. The teachers loved and bragged about me that he'd do anything just to ruin it for me and see it all crumble right in front of my face. You could tell just by the look on his face that he hated that with a passion although he was the only one in class that seemed to have had a problem with that in particular.

I experienced a lot of hate from kids my age growing up and being that I did, I'm surprised I didn't kill myself right on the spot, although I can't lie and say it didn't cross my mind then because kids can say some of the meanest, most hurtful shit in the books that crossed their minds. I was called ugly, gay, and nobody ever liked me at all because of who I am. I would always get rated low in the class when it came to the girls rating all of us guys based on our looks, and people wrote "ugly" beside my year book pictures as well. I know for a fact that I looked better than half those kids in the year book. I felt like I was at my lowest point, to the extent of killing myself like slitting my wrist or just hanging myself on the ceiling fan.

My grandparents didn't even know that I went through this kind of situation when I was a child. I kept a lot of it bottled up, so they only knew the basics of what someone else would tell them based of what they see. Describing the type of hell that I had to endure back then changes me into who I am today. It sometimes causes me to overreact in a situation where I feel like I am being attacked or confronted.

I was able to carry what I went through for so long in my heart, a lot of people may say that I'm harsh or rude whenever I talk to them. Sometimes I'm a little too blunt which is for me it was only a reaction based on how I was treated before. It seems as if I was forced to change my way of thought from the way I used to get treated because I felt like a punching bag. If only they experienced what I went through back then, then they would understand how hard it carried over into my adult life today. Those things I experienced when I was as a child to the way kids call me all of those things today were still very hurtful to hear. It's like people making fun at me because of that, and I never really understood why. This not only made me feel unwanted but how I viewed myself back then makes no difference at all since I have always been compared to others. They'd also talk about my weight and about how chubby I had gotten because my metabolism slowed down and I had gained a little weight compared to the other guys. Part of me eating was like that depression that I had to how I looked which made me eat a lot more and put on more weight.

It hurt me so bad, so I'm down on my knees and ask God why do I look this way, but I'm glad I didn't let none of what the other kids would say, take control of me or define who I am as a person today because had I done so, I would've missed out on a lot, based off a bunch of irrelevant opinions that I couldn't change just to satisfy others. One day, I had to take a look in the mirror and tell myself that I am enough regardless of what people may think of me. I'm good enough to pick myself back up and keep on moving and marching to the beat of my own drum. It was always something back then, even though my looks didn't mature as fast as the other guys do.

Even now in my early twenties transitioning to my mid-twenties, I still look younger and facial hairs are still not growing yet. At first, that was something I started feeling insecure about, but then I had to tell myself not to worry about something as such because that just means that I'm going to age well a lot less compared to a lot of people who actually do look their age now. I've always been more mature than most guys and even girls seemed to overlook it.

Being raised by older people most definitely gave me this "old soul" and this spark of wisdom that I tend to carry with me now because I don't really like to go clubbing and do a lot of things that people in my age does. I figured that if you go to the club, you're looking for trouble because that's where a lot of people like to cause a lot of commotion, and stuff tends to pop off in a negative way. I thank God daily for giving me the strength that he did to deal with some of those things that I had to endure because it made me a stronger and much more resilient, strong- minded person people see right before their very eyes today that's slowly learning how to stand on his own two feet.

You can say that the challenges I had to face while growing up had to be one of the most difficult and biggest impacts of my life, but I steady count it all joy even when I felt as if I lost it all and have to start over again. I went through this phase of not loving myself for who I was. I feel like no woman would ever love me because she will be ashamed to even sit and talk with me due to all the negative things life has brought me then. That is also the reason why I didn't choose to surround myself with those types of people. It's not like I asked for that kind of hate but, I just received it and it somehow stumbled over into my adult life now. I catch shade every now and then, which is why I became a homebody and stayed away from people because my reaction won't be what others may expect from when we were kids. I questioned my appearance, my demeanor, my posture, just about everything about myself to the fact that I couldn't live my life and truly be happy the way that I wanted to be. I'm so hesitant on showing off my true self because I was trying to hide my imperfections because I was so unhappy of how I look physically. I would always try to keep myself in nice clothes that would fit loose on me because I felt that tighter clothes would make me look even bigger than I was when the bigger clothes were making me look even more heavy set.

As I looked in the mirror one day, I saw how big this one shirt made me look like I was huge, and it made me change my whole thought process and start to find clothes that fit my body type more although I would still be insecure about it in the long run because I felt as if I still had something to hide. People would say I had a sense of style back then, but I always felt like I was this chubby, fat kid that stuck out more than the other guys because of the extra weight I carried on me and I couldn't seem to lose any of it for nothing, no matter how hard I tried. I thought people would low-key talk about me and whisper things with each other, which I'm pretty sure some of them did because that's just how people were. But all of this happened a little later when I entered High School.

As time went on, my cousin whom I caught up with in first grade left me again and went to second grade which made me have to repeat the first grade as well. I was so ashamed because I failed twice and it pushed me back another year, making me feel like I was either dumb or just plain slow to catch up with what the teachers were talking about in class and sometimes, I just didn't pay close enough attention because school was one of the last places I would've much rather been in. It seemed like every time I fail a grade, I would get this long lecture about why I should've paid more attention in class before so I won't be left behind. I always told my mama and the rest of them that I failed because I figured she had this high expectation for me and I failed her yet again.

As a mother, I knew she wanted nothing but the best for me and to also see me succeed in everything that I do because she went above and beyond when it comes to me in order to make sure I didn't want for anything, especially out of all her grandkids. I know it had to be disappointing to her to have to watch me repeat another grade yet again.

Things started to get better for me as I got older though, but when I was younger, school just wasn't my forte, and I couldn't seem to get with all the work we had to do for about seven long dreadful hours of the day. I looked at everybody around me and thought to myself, "How did I let them leave me and get so far behind the way that I did? For a very long time, I was lost as a child because there are so many things going through my head. Mentally I went through a lot of difficulties. During our class, I'm afraid to speak up and express my feelings without being judged since I felt I'm a bit slower than the others. Some of my classmates easily get by and learned from the lessons taught. Being in this type of situation would make anybody question themselves about any little thing that they do; plus I was already getting picked on, so I didn't want to add anything else to the fire in order to make it worse than what it already was. This played a big factor in how I viewed myself because I couldn't be an average child the way I wanted to be back then. I eventually got to that point where I felt like I was illiterate and couldn't learn a thing as long as it was school related, and if I did catch on, I'd forget it right off the bat if we weren't constantly going through it repeatedly in order to refresh our minds right before a test. But it was one subject that played a big part into how I performed academically. I've been an honor student before but not as consistent compared with the other students. I think I have a learning disability since I can't easily get by on the lessons taught and with that, I am again disappointed with myself. As everyone in the class huddled around each other to see what one another had, I wanted to be nosey and see what grades everyone else had without showing mine to anybody because I felt like they'd be judging me yet again based on how I was performing, so I hid mines in my bag. I got compared with people so much when it came to looks or how I acted or dressed that I didn't want it to be the same way when it came to my grades, even though I was actually doing better than a few of the others.

6

The She Wolf

A few years later, as I approached the fourth grade, I was steadily catching up with a few of the kids that were my age. I had started with from the beginning who would always use to make fun of me on how I failed a couple of grades before they did. They took the state standardized tests that every student had to pass when reaching that certain grade level, and if not, they would automatically be retained unless they went to summer school to try and make it up.

There was this one girl who I came back in contact with because she was one of those that failed the test, causing her to have to repeat the grade again since she didn't go or finish summer school. She was known as a class clown and she laughed at almost anything that she thought was funny whether it was something about sex or anything funny. I thought it was kind of odd when you mentioned something related to sex considering that we are still in grade school.

This person had been like a close friend of mine ever since we met back when I first started school, although I always found myself getting into some kind of trouble at school when dealing with her, and it kind of made my reputation as one of the good students go down the drain because it seemed like everything I did got me into a world of trouble. She would always have her shady ways toward me; for whatever reason it was whenever we both got into trouble and put out of the class for something that she did and me for laughing and going along with it like a dumbass. She told everyone that I am the reason why she didn't make it to the next grade level. As what others said that in previous years, she had this record of being good in bad-mouthing and cursing other teachers. That was the first time that I have been accused since we've been good friends before.

I recall a time when she talked about an elder lady who came and subbed for the class, and we both got in trouble for what she said about the lady. I didn't really have a lot of friends back then and I honestly didn't even know if this person was my friend like she claimed to be from the actions that she showed to me on a daily basis.

I wasn't too big on sports and didn't really know how to play all of them except a few because I was so insecure and self-conscious about running in front of others, so we started hanging around each other, and then I got that label as one of those students who act out in class and get in trouble all the time, being an all-time troublemaker from our laughing all the time, disrupting the class and I didn't understand because some stuff wasn't even that deep for us to get in trouble, but because she was this goofy person that pretty much laughed at any and everything, it was always a problem. I didn't approve of a lot of the things that she had done, but I didn't say anything because I already knew how she was and I didn't have time to be going back and forth. It wasn't anything major, but the teachers known me as a good student who literally never did anything or had never gotten into any trouble.

When I started hanging around the wrong people, they started to think otherwise, which led into me staying in trouble with any little thing I did in class even if I smiled the wrong the wrong way. It then got to the point of where I would get put in ISS (in-school suspension) right along with her, just for the simplest thing like laughing because they always thought we were this troubled package that came together. It's like they thought that when one gets in trouble, the other one should get in trouble as well. This led all the way until it was time for us to take the school's standardized test that we had to pass or else we were going to spend our summer in school, trying to make up for what we didn't do throughout the year.

When taking the test, I honestly didn't take it all that serious like I should've and so didn't many others because a lot of them would finish way before the timer even rung. I was one of those slow test-takers since I am the only one left during the examination day while others are done. I would rush through the rest of it without a care in the world as to whether it was even right or not in the first place, or the teacher would call out the time remaining, and I would just go mark the answers to fill them in just so I didn't leave anything blank.

Fast-forward to the end of the school year when we all got our test scores back, which was a whole different story because I wasn't too thrilled with the results I got back. All those marking answers down led to me failing one part of the school's state-required tests, which was the math section that I wasn't surprised by because I sucked at math, causing me to have to spend my summer going to summer school with a bunch of my other classmates that failed the test right along with me. That pretty much meant that we had to get up early every morning like we were going to regular school, so we didn't really have much of a summer like the ones that passed the test the first time around. Plus, there were some high school students that had to go too, and my brother was one of them.

There were so many thoughts going through my head because I knew I was going to fail that test from the jump even if I had took my time like I was supposed to. The girl that I stayed in trouble with throughout the school year actually passed her tests that time around because it was her second time in the same grade, so she knew what to do then. But then again, I believe they passed her because they got tired of seeing her in the first place and didn't want to keep holding her back. I heard an earful from one of my older cousins because she already knew how she was when it came down to the girl getting into trouble and having the disrespectful mouth and nasty attitude that she had.

When the classes took course over the summer, I was put into a class where I didn't know anybody except one person. She was considered to be like my secret girlfriend at the time because she didn't tease me like the other girls did and she actually liked me for who I was.

After that summer, everyone got their results already, not knowing if they would be promoted to the next grade or not. I felt all types of emotions at that time and I'm not sure if I can make it to the next level. But what I'm sure of was I did my best and if things won't go well then it's fine. When I finally got the results in my hand, I just stood there, feeling cold and I can hardly breathe. When I opened the results to see what score I made, words couldn't express how I feel way back then. I've been thinking that maybe things might go well or might not.

Finally, after opening the letter, I saw where it said I passed on the test, promoting me to the next grade, which had me in complete shock because I didn't really think I was going to pass it that time around either, and the ones that didn't pass the test the second time was promoted just because they kept going and it was this law back then of NCLB (No Child Left Behind) at the time as well. I was already two grades behind in school, so test taking was not something that I was good at, making me feel like school was not for me and I was only attending because my mama was making me go, otherwise, I would've been stopped going.

Back in my younger years, I had always felt like it was a waste of my time because I got sick and tired of the worrying so much and the constant fear of not knowing what to do next. It would always drain and stress the hell out of me to the fullest that I felt like my brain could hardly function or think critically when I'm dealing with difficult problems. That by itself, would always have me in for an earful. I was always told that I overthink any situation that I'm in, and I make it even more difficult and complicated than what it has to be, especially when given a task that I seem to know nothing of and I completely freeze up on. Even now, when I'm faced with something that I don't know too much about, I freeze up, not knowing exactly what to do next, so I would wait to get another person's opinion on it before moving forward.

After getting the results back from our tests about a week in advance, school started in full force later that month of August, and I found myself back into the same shenanigans with the same person I was during the last school year. My behavior problem started all over again like I haven't learned my lessons before. It even turned into her trying to bully me as well from asking me for money like every single day to just doing little things to get under my skin on purpose, like she was supposed to have some sort of control over me and in what I do I couldn't keep money on me for anything trying to keep her friends even though she lied about it. Back then, I thought that I need to have somebody else besides me until school pass by smoothly so I won't feel bored. At the time, it felt like she was filling that void of mine that I had during school hours that nobody else could understand but her, but I hurting myself in the long run because I received the short end of the stick. It all started that current year when we first got back together for the first time since elementary and became hell from there. Little did I know what I was getting myself into for that matter or how she maneuvered her sneaky way through because had I known, I would've never gone down that path with her knowing she was already showing the signs after a couple weeks of school, and they always say that when a person shows you who they are, believe them. It's like I went through this phase in my life as a kid, trying to please other people who didn't give a damn about me, and I was so torn because I didn't know how to say no or when to draw that line like I do now in my adulthood.

The person that I am today is just fed up with people's bull shit and how I was treated, so now when I feel like people are coming for my character, I strike right back of how I used to feel. It's like my mind instantly reverts to my early childhood stages and I used to ask myself all the time why people had to step on my self-esteem because it gave me a different view on how I look at people and how I love women because they were the main ones judging and comparing me when no need for that.

Growing up is difficult, it seems like if I let everybody control my life and dictate whatever they want. I look back at things like this and ask myself, "How did I even let it get to that moment of weakness and vulnerability to where I just wanted to shed some tears and kill myself all by the way that I looked and the stuff that people would say?"

The person I am today is a lot better and older now and won't tolerate anyone to rule my life again. I was a helpless child before who was afraid to speak up, lack of self-confidence, but now I am comfortable to share with everyone who I am today. We don't think about those things at the time because we were kids who just wanted to have fun and didn't want to feel like an outcast, but all along, I became the person that I feared just by trying to avoid the problem, instead of trying to attack it head-on. This occurred quite often and it went on for quite some time because I was always giving her my money time and time again, and she still didn't seem to be satisfied.

At this moment, I didn't seem to care because I just wanted her to be happy even if she didn't feel the same way. She even threatened me that she didn't want to be my friend anymore. She always gets mad at me and says bad things against me. It hurts me and it turns out that I need to avoid her. She even embarrassed me in front of a lot of people, and I still kept coming back like it didn't bother or me at all.

At the end of school year, she got so upset with me for like no reason. I asked her what was wrong or did I do something that caused her to become even more upset.

When I asked her that, she physically hit me a couple of times and tossing me onto the ground like I was a piece of shit. Everybody just looked at us at the time but didn't really say anything but "Get up. Don't let her do you like that!" But if I had hit her, that would've been a different story, so I just kept my hands to myself and acted accordingly. So I got up and fix myself first and paused for a while. I have intentions on hitting her but I realized that there is no need to do that since she's a girl and she's with her brother at that time.

Now, I didn't even hit the girl back because she was a female, so I didn't touch. Now, had I laid my hands on her that would've made me look less of a man, so I just sat there and took what she did to me, which was embarrassing for me in front of the entire class. She put me in a headlock and tossed me around several times and slung me back on the floor. She couldn't fight worth nothing but, in her mind, I bet she thought she was doing something, so I just let her.

Once the fight was over, the substitute teacher that we had sent both of us to the principal's office even though I wasn't in the wrong for any of that. While sitting in the office, the principal didn't even come out while she was talking to the secretary. All I heard her say was "Suspend both of them home!" I didn't know how to react to a situation such as that because it was my first time ever getting suspended from school, which I thought it was unfair because I didn't even do anything to the girl. All I did was ask her, "What's wrong?" and a psychical altercation led from her putting her hands on me. The whole class sided with me because they knew that she hit me first although some acted if though they didn't see that she hit me trying to stay neutral in the situation, but I mean right is right and wrong is wrong in my book. Plus, they knew I didn't bother anybody and she had the reputation of constantly getting into trouble. We were both only like twelve years old at the time with her being just a few months older than me. But it didn't really matter, so we both got three days of suspension right at the end of the year. I was praying that it didn't affect both our GPAs. I didn't want that one of us to fail just because of what happened. I guess that's the price you pay when dealing with people who doesn't have much to lose, or they just don't care or think about the consequences they could be putting you or themselves in afterward.

Being in that situation made me realize that I should put things in perspective, evaluate myself and the people that I chose to hang around. The way she humiliated me in public made me look as if I was her punching bag whenever she got mad. I was dealing with a lot of things back then; I had lost my grandpa eight months ago, prior to that my cousin got stabbed in the neck. Good thing that I still have my grandma who helped me recover from all the hardships. I remember that my grandpa started getting really sickly and losing his strength to the point where he couldn't really do anything for himself, so the best option for him at the time was to go into the hospital for a little while until he could regain his strength again.

Even as just a child, I could sense that something wasn't right and could tell his health was slowly fading away because he couldn't do things for himself like he normally could, and I know that had to take a toll on him after a while because he was so used to doing things his way without the help of someone else. I knew something was getting ready to happen soon. I just couldn't pinpoint what it was, but I had that feeling way before it happened. Fast-forward to about another week, I walk in the house to the news that he passed away that morning while we were in school. Tears suddenly started to roll down my face from the devastation by the news I had just received, I didn't know what to do because I was hurt and didn't expect to hear something of that sort. He worked my nerves when he was here, but one thing I can say is that he truly was a provider to many of us in so many ways, and for that, I take that with me and the years full of wisdom he bestowed upon me. Then there was the unexpected tragic incident that hit us all when my cousin got killed at a party that was hosted in our hometown. I remember our small city having some of the best parties there was, but I was never allowed to go because of how overprotective my grandma was when it came to me going out.

While I was still trying to cope with the heartbreaking tragedy that struck out family from those two deaths in particular. We got passed it like a family should had because we had our differences then, just not separated like we are now. Everyone was eventually able to move pass what was going on as time proceeded its way through. We then began to heal and move on from everything that had took place, although I could tell that left a weary look on my grandmother's face. We then started another school year but nobody was informed that we only had one teacher teaching the class the entire school year, so both classes were combined into one in a little red building. It had to be about forty of students in one little building, but we managed to get by and make the best of it. I went back from being that troubled student in class to the good student again because I didn't really just talk to anybody that much and I started hanging with guys a bit more but I much rather preferred to be by myself. Me and the girl would make eye contact with each other over the past year but would never really say anything to each other because of how she did me that last year before we got out.

Close to the end of that year, we were put into groups of five, and she was in my group, which had been kind of awkward because we hadn't spoken since that past year before she tossed me around like I was a salad. After finally being in the group and the both of us talking to everybody else but each other, she finally acknowledged the fact that what she did was wrong and sincerely apologized in a letter and that she would never do me like that again. I didn't know what to expect because it's like I didn't want anything else to do with her. I had been at peace and trouble free again since we stopped talking to one another. With me being the type of person that I was, I thought it was a good thing that she could acknowledge the fact that what she did was wrong and was willing to sincerely apologize for it. We started our regular conversations again, but I wasn't going to let her get me into any more trouble by laughing and joking around with her because I wasn't trying be that trouble maker anymore and she understood that because she didn't get into any trouble that year as well. I'm not sure if it was because she knew this teacher in particular wouldn't tolerate what her behavior compared to the others or that she just simply had the utmost respect for this one because she never gave her any trouble. Our seventh grade year was slightly different because we both got into trouble, but in different classes because we had a schedule where we had seven different classes and each teacher taught two of them except the P.E. teacher. She wasn't bullying me and asking me for money anymore, and I didn't get in trouble as much as she did but we stayed getting put out the class right along with a lot more people. With us different teachers throughout the day like high school students, although we were only in junior high made it easier for me to. We would always get in trouble in our math class by mouthing off at the teacher, but we weren't the only two who would get into trouble and put out of the classroom when it came to this specific teacher. Everybody in class just about got put out, which would be funny to see because of how red the man got in the face when we pissed him off or either aggravated him to a certain extent.

The school's first and last academic decathlon came around where they would take the four smartest students in our class, and they would compete against the other seventh grade class to see who would win. One person would also be the understudy for each class. Everyone in each grade got to compete with one another to see who would win the competition. The rest of us sat in the stadium to support our classmates who were competing against each other. Throughout the academic decathlon, my classmates and I started acting up, laughing, and clowning around each other. The teacher told us to be quiet but we all laughed at him. My classmates kept on teasing him which hilariously so I laughed right along with them. In my mind I was like, they didn't have to disrespect the man like that, but people will be people. He got so red in the face and embarrassed till he sent just about our whole class to ISS (in-school suspension) except for the ones competing and the understudy. We piled the few desks in one little office and sat there until it was time to go home and were told that we had to come back the next day for disrupting the people and our classmates competing. While sitting in there, we had to write, "I will not disrupt the school's decathlon no more," or something of that sort about one thousand times that our hands started to cramp. We didn't have it too bad in there because the ISS teacher was cool. She was the mother of my classmate, she's cool in the first place and she's not strict at all.

The few classmates that didn't get into trouble have a party thrown for them by our homeroom teacher while the rest of us felt played because she would've never thrown that party if the whole class hadn't gotten in trouble, but we didn't too much care anyway. We basically sat there, writing for the majority of the day until about twelve that noon when she told us all to stop writing, which was a relief because my hands were beginning to feel like they were about to fall off from all that writing she was having us do.

After the break, the school year started and proceeded through the year with us having a fun day just for the students, leading all the way up to my cousin and brother's graduation since they were the last actual class graduating from our home school. Now, it was last year that my home school became a grade school and junior high school. This was back in the year of 2009, so one of my older cousins and brothers were the luckiest to graduate from our home school. The rest of us are transferring to another school which is only thirty minutes away. I did get to stay at our home school another year later after that because I was in eighth grade then, so it didn't apply to others although some still switched schools in the first place. We had two other choices then, but the majority of us chose to stay where we were at already while the rest decided to go see what the other schools were about. We had fun that last year. We assisted kids since we were in the oldest grade.

We had the standardized state test that we should take which was the same test we took when we were in fourth-graders, but it was a more advanced high school level of schoolwork. One of our teachers assigned us a state test tutor who could help us prepare for the test so that we would pass and not have to go to summer school. Most of us dreaded taking that test even more because we remembered how it was back in the earlier grade. The tutor was very friendly and hands on when it came to helping us pass the test. She had us identifying the key words in the math constructed response questions that could possibly help us pass the class.

The week came for us to take the test with me not feeling my best. I tried to push through to finish taking the test for the rest of that day with my classmates but because I had gotten really sick that weekend before, that caused me to take only the first half of the test, and I then checked out of school afterwards and returned later that week to finish the rest of it on my own. I was put into the classroom next door, so I wouldn't have any distractions, so I could finish the test without any disturbance. It didn't take me long to finish, so I headed to my next class right after that. I have that confidence that I passed the test but I still have that feeling of doubt because I knew I didn't take the test well.

A couple of months later, the results came in and everyone was nervous and shook about their scores, especially me, and we couldn't find out what we had unless a parent of ours came up to the school to pick up ours results. I snuck my phone out and called my grandma to have somebody come pick up my scores because I really wanted to know what I made on the test.

A few minutes later, I saw one of my aunts pulling up to the school, so I ran up the sidewalk and into the office to see what I had. When they told me that I passed three of the four tests and that I passed the two main portions that actually count, it was like a big relief off my shoulders, and I knew my grandmother's as well because we didn't want to go through the hassle of getting stuff for summer school. I think I was shocked more than anything because I somewhat had that feeling that I failed that test, but God is still good to me and answered all my prayers. Once I got my results, the rest of the class got theirs as well, and the majority of us passed the test and left just a few to have to go to summer school.

7
Surviving High School

The year was slowly coming to an end, and we knew that was our last few days of walking around that hall of our home school were coming to an end. We already knew we were getting ready to go into something way different from what we were used with tons of other people we'd know nothing about and I honestly didn't know how to react to a situation of that sort, considering my self-esteem. Everything was new to me at that time. I didn't know what to expect at all as well. Since the school was so big, I need to for direction and ask someone on how to get there.

    The other people I used to be so close to back in my elementary days had drifted apart because everybody was trying to find who they were, and a lot of us that separated within that year had some sort of disconnect like we really didn't know how to talk to each other anymore, then you had the ones that tried to keep up with the crowd and hang out and I just wasn't that type to try and be something that I'm not. This was where reality started to hit me all at once because we were mixed in with a group of people I had no choice but get to know them, so I really felt like more of an outcast and struggled my hardest to find who I was because High School was pretty tough for me and it made me feel isolated from everybody that I came across. I hardly had class with anybody that I knew, so that really made me stay to myself because I didn't participate in any sports and it put me in a difficult place to find that specific group of people I could possibly talk to. I felt like the odds were stacked against me, and I dreaded getting up every morning, knowing I would have to get up and go to a different school that wasn't the school that I grew up in. People looked at me mad whenever I got off the bus, like, "Who does this dude think he is?" I wasn't hanging around my cousin at that time because we hardly ever saw each other except in the morning."

I was mostly by myself because they would always put us in two different lunch shifts which would aggravate me because I didn't have much of a social life. I struggled with this for a long time in my life because I've always felt like something was wrong with me, which caused me to put up a wall with people to block out what I was feeling. Luckily, I had some more other people who came from the same place I came from, who were there for me during that difficult time. We sat on the bench outside every day and just chilled, so I didn't feel lonesome during the throughout the years I was there because we always ended up on the same lunch shift. I knew where I stood with a lot of people I came from the same place because they would walk pass me and act like I wasn't there, but it didn't bother me because I expected it. Some people would always talk about me, whether it was about the clothes I had on or how I looked and the faces that I made just because my teeth grew back unevenly, so my bottom lip shifted out a tad bit more than my top lip did.

Experiencing all of that as early in my life as often I did made me want to keep to myself even to this day because people can say some of the most hurtful shit they could think of without even considering how you feel about the situation. I didn't really communicate with a lot of the people whom I stayed in the same city with, and we would get up and go to the same school every morning and wouldn't say anything to each other.

There are times that I feel like I'm out of place, but because of that, I felt that being who I am as a person, who I wanted to be and how I view certain things and put them into perspective as well. I focused on nothing but my school work since I didn't really have any friends and the few that I did have, we would see each other occasionally aside from the ones I had on the same lunch shift as me. My grades went up because I was so focused on myself at that time that nothing else mattered within that moment.

Life's Scars and Wisdom

On the first day in class, this loud, obnoxious girl walked in the room, being all loud like she owned the school coming in telling people what to do. I being different from the other student didn't pay any attention to her at that time. She didn't know me either but she was so rude to me and I don't know how to handle it. We had our differences like I had my differences with other guys in the class who would throw paper at me for always going to class and not skipping like they did. They either smoked or dipped outside of class and behind the buildings where no teacher wouldn't think to look for them to quick. They'd sit in the back of the classroom while I sat in front, and they would throw paper at me continuously until one day, I finally snapped on them. Me and one of the guys almost got into a fight in class until the teacher stepped in front of me and said, "I'll take care of him. You got too much going on to these immature little boys to mess that up."

It was a relief that she stepped in and said that to me because a part of me wanted to beat the hell out of him, but she wouldn't let me because of the consequences I would had to suffer even though it would've been my first offense. That was only half my worries when dealing with the guys because I got into it with the loudmouthed girl who talked all throughout class. She threw shade at me on a daily basis, so when she posted a picture on Facebook, I simply made a comment about her nose in a joking way, and she took it the wrong way and came at me though my inbox, calling me ugly, same-clothes wearing, and crooked teeth. Those are the words that I usually heard from anyone else whenever they got into trouble. just basically trying to step on my self-esteem and making me feel lower than how I already felt. Back then, my self-esteem was already damaged, so it wasn't nothing more she could've said that was going to hurt me at that point. After going back and forth for about an hour or two through Facebook, she then told me to look for her brother the next morning. None of that mattered to me because I already knew how she was and she caused any kinds of scene like she would normally do. Then there was this engineering class I got stuck taking where we had to construct on how to put things together. I wasn't really all that familiar with the class, but I knew the teacher because she was one of my brother and cousin's teacher back at our old school, so I knew who she was, and she knew exactly who I was when I first stepped into the class. I didn't care too much for her and gave her a run for her money because every little thing she said to me in class, I came back with a smart remark, whether she wanted me to interact and engage in class assignments, I just knew I wasn't having it and she already knew how I was coming. I didn't know anybody in that class really but one of my friends and she was basically the only one I communicated with because I didn't know anybody else, nor did I care to. She would always tell me every day before entering the class to behave myself because she already knew what I was going to do if the teacher said anything to me that was out of the way. I went in class and laid my head on the desk because I didn't know any of the material. To me, it seemed like it was on some college-type-level work and pretty much everybody else that I was in the class with were honor students, so they were like a bunch of nerds including my friend, who knew how to do the work and helped each other. Some students were like me and couldn't fully grasp the information, but I was just more vocal and didn't really care but they just had someone else in the class who knew how to do it, do it for them. My friend would do her best to try and help me on certain occasions, but she even started changing on me to try to please some guy she was interested in. The back and forth between the engineering teacher and I went on and on for the longest time because I just couldn't bring myself to do that hard level of work that I couldn't seem to understand. It's like everything that I was going through was shaping me into this cold person around the heart who didn't care too much about anything. My outspoken personality is what makes me who I am today, although people constantly try to tell me now that I need to watch what I say because I could offend the wrong person, but the reason I am the way that I am is because didn't nobody tip toe around my feelings or cared to hear me out, so I dish it how it was done to me. I find myself having these flashback moments of how I even got to this point in my, that's why I tell people that if I have something to say, best believe I'll say it with no hesitation or thinking about it. Every day when I got to the class, I ended up laying my head on my desk because she always wants me to participate in the class, and I gave her the passive look. I had this killer facial expression even when I didn't try to, and people would notice it right off the bat. Some people tell me to this day that my facial expression looks mean or that I'm upset about something even when I don't try to be. It's like I had this scowl look on my face that I made. My bottom lip would always shift out, which made a lot of folks talk about me. After she called me out in front of the class one too many times, it started to rub me the wrong way, so I told her what was on my mind and what I thought about her, especially after she tried to compare me to my own brother because that's one thing that you don't do. I may have been disrespectful, but she was disrespecting me because he and I were two totally different people in school. There was no need for her to bring him up the way that she did not at all for that matter. He was more of a calm, follow-the-crowd type of person while I always tried to avoid being seen. She told me that I was nothing like him and that I should act more like him, and maybe, I'll get far in life and stop having that I-don't-care attitude what she called it because it's not cute. Not that I had that bad attitude then, I just didn't care too much for her or her teaching skills and I let it be known. It's like she showed more favoritism to the honor students than us regular students which she said was not the case when I confronted her, but I still think it was. Right before we got out for the holidays, she had one of the most disrespectful attitudes towards me, and I guess she was fed up with me, so she sent me to the principal's office, thinking I was gone get into trouble. But when I got in there, the principal was shocked to see me walk through the door. Her words were, "You're in here? You don't even do anything!" I said, "My point exactly." She just told me to sit down and wait until it's time to go because it was a half a day anyway.

    I stayed in the office and helped them out and laughed about the whole situation because I wasn't a troubled student, and by the time I got in high school, I calmed completely down from how I used to be. At the end of the semester, report cards were in, and I passed her class with a C. Till this day, I still wonder how I got that C because most of my work in her class was incomplete or wrong. I think she just passed me because she felt sorry for me and didn't want to teach me for that second half that upcoming semester. Going through so many ups and downs in life that, I had to be able to pick myself back up when needed to and bounce back from what I was going through. After the death of my grandpa back in 2006, I knew that my grandmother wasn't always going to be around, so I started transitioning in my life as I got older but I always had some sort of setback in the process of that. The year after that, my cousins and some of the people I started out in school with became juniors in high school, and that was when my whole mind-set about school slowly started to change and took a turn toward the right direction. I started taking these classes online called Education 2020, short for E2020, so that I could catch up with them since I was considered a sophomore. I didn't really take it serious in the beginning because I stayed in one class that whole school year, but with me being so far behind on a lot of other classes, I had to work extra hard that summer to get to where I wanted to be in order to graduate with them the year after that. I just so happened to finish the class I spent my whole sophomore year on. By the end of the year, my cousins were having their ring ceremony to becoming seniors for the next upcoming school year. I went to have a talk with the school's secretary and librarian, who were over the whole Education 2020 program for students trying to graduate early or got behind and graduate on time. I sat them down and told them, I needed to come out of school the next upcoming school year and they could see how serious I was. I got tired of being behind the people I very first started school with school and I was determined I was going to graduate with them. These ladies came through for me in the end because I stayed on the honor roll up until I got into the program good and that went flying out the window. They told me that it's possible that if I were to take online classes to cover up my junior year, I would more than likely graduate with my cousins that next school year, but I have to be consistent when ding it. I had to put in a lot of time and hard work during that summer of 2012 to get to where they were. All the blood, sweat, and tears made me want to just give up overall because it seemed like it was just beginning to be too much for me. The many sleepless nights I stayed up making sure that my work was finished before going to bed, missing out on a s lot of activities that were taken place. I worked day in and day out nonstop on online classes that entire summer where I mentally didn't know if I was going or coming. I barely went outside or had any time for myself because I worked on classes 24/7 nonstop and it started to overwhelm me la bit. I worked myself so much to the point of where I started to give up because I thought God had given up on me, but in the back of my mind, I knew that it would be all worth it in the end, so I pushed myself day in and day out to get through what seemed to be one of the most difficult times in my life. I stressed out, barely ate anything, and didn't go anywhere for less than an hour or two because I knew I had to get to get back to what I was doing, because it isn't like anyone else was going to do it for me. I went from one class online to another while they were doubling up on me in just a short amount of time. It only took me a week to finish each class with a total number of about eleven classes overall done online within that current summer before it was time to go back to school. Once I was done, I had a test prep classes I took online because it was a state standardized test that I didn't pass like a year or two before that. They were so impressed with the number of classes I had done in that short amount of time, that they stated that I was the only student in history who attempted that many classes and actually passed everything that fast because nobody else had took that many classes and excelled. It was a moment of feeling proud that I actually could finish that many classes in that short amount of time before the new school year even started. Once the new school year came around, I was classified as a whole senior with my cousins instead of being a junior. Another close personal friend of mines who I was cool with at the time being, wasn't too pleased with the decision I was making at first, by me graduating a year earlier because she felt like I was leaving her behind, but that was something I had to do for myself at that point in time, so finally came to an understanding because they were in their right grade or just a year behind and not two like I was. Once I finished doing those all those classes online, it made me appear as only a year behind and it was such a good feeling to know that I worked my ass to be where I was and those sleepless nights finally paid off. Later that year, my friend threw this extravagant party for her eighteenth birthday where everybody was drinking and having a good time. She invited people that we went to school with to come check the party out and see what it was about. It's like she was always trying to stay in competition with somebody when it was no need for that but that's just how some people were. I sat in the corner to myself and just watched everyone else dance, trying to be cool like the other guys were because I knew someone would have something to say if I stepped outside my comfort zone for a minute. I've always thought I had more personality than other guys because they always pretended to be this cool macho type while I was a bit more on the outspoken side but would sometimes keep everything bottled up, so no one would have this misconception of me.

That same month, I was getting ready to take senior portraits and I had this feeling, I just couldn't pinpoint exactly what it was during that time. I was so overwhelmed because I did my part but I still fail. I had to retake the math part of the standardized test because that was the only part of the test. I couldn't seem to get pass the math portion of the test to save my life. What threw me off is that it was right before graduation when they called us over the intercom to come retake the test. With me feeling the way that I was, I had a feeling it was going to come back and bite me in my ass, but I didn't care at that moment, even though state rules are that if you don't get a certain score on the state's standardized test, you won't walk with your class. Math was like my weakest subject in school and I had always had trouble with it, but I somehow managed to pass the course but the exact test until a little later on. I could basically have A's and B's in everything else and C's on my transcript when it came to math, except for Algebra I, where I surprisingly had an A.

The graduate sales people came to our school to get everything situated for graduation back in January. Everyone ordered their invitations, cap and gowns, and other extra items that they chose to get to help celebrate that momentous occasion. I just chose my cap and gown and a hoodie with the year I graduated on it because it was like something in the back of my mind then was telling me I wasn't gone graduate, so don't waste any money on any of the irrelevant stuff. It's like I knew in the back of my head that something wasn't right before May even got there, but I played it out smooth to see what was going to happen. I failed two parts of that standardized test online, which was the EOC (end of course) test for the science and mathematics part, both in Algebra I and Geometry. I passed the science part the second time around with no trouble, so that was out the way. As for both math parts, I didn't have much luck when it came to both of those because of my weakness. I had to pass either Algebra I or Geometry to be completely done with the whole test overall, but unfortunately, I didn't in the end. I'm thinking I at least passed one of them because I never got my score back from what I had made in December until the end of that year, so I had to retake the algebra part again in May before the seniors even got out of school.

The year slowly started winding down, and everyone was getting ready for graduation. The seniors last day was May 9, 2013. Not to mention, I had just left from that morning class at like nine o'clock that morning right after that class. The next week came, and I was having a good time waiting for graduation that Friday because I thought I was in the clear on things, but something still didn't seem right to me. My gut feeling told me that something was wrong the whole time, but I simply didn't care. You know how you get that gut reaction that something isn't right, but you still go along with it anyway? That's the feeling that I had to endure during that process.

That following Tuesday afternoon, I checked my phone and seen I had a missed phone call and a voicemail from the school's secretary. In the back of my mind, I already knew what it was about before calling back. I unlocked my phone to listen to the voicemail before calling back, and she said that I need to call her back as soon as possible regarding my test scores on the EOC test. Once I built up enough nerve, I then called back, and she told me that I need to come take the geometry part of the test because I didn't score high enough to pass the algebra back in December. Keep in mind that I took the algebra part again the week before the seniors got out and still didn't pass it like I had thought I did. I found a ride and rushed over to the school after hours to take the remaining test because graduation was that Friday and that was Tuesday she called me to let me know what was going on with that situation. I had to take the test that day in order to receive the test results back before the day of graduation to know whether or not I was going walk with my class.

I waited anxiously those two days, hoping that I had passed that test, but deep down, I knew I didn't pass it because that part was just as hard as the algebra. But somehow, I was just ready to hear the news that I didn't, so that I could stop tensing up and worrying so much about it. This is why to this day, I know to trust my gut reaction to anything because it has never stirred me in the wrong direction.

I finally pulled myself together and waited for the counselor to call and tell me what I had already known but just needed confirmation. As the text came through, I was nervous about opening it because I already knew what the outcome was going to be and that was just what it was. I opened up the text, and it said, "I am so sorry, but you did not pass the test which means you cannot walk with your class the next day." Feeling so empty after reading that text, I didn't know what to do or who to be mad at or why was I even born because it seemed like nothing went right in my life.

I started asking God why I had to be placed in a situation like that. I didn't understand like why it had to be the way that it was and needed answers as to why every bad thing would happen to me in life, not just school related. A part of me felt broken, cracked, and shattered into a million pieces because it seemed like something so precious was getting taken away from me at that moment that I knew I could never get back.

8

Closing My Dreadful High School Life

I woke up that morning the day of graduation on May 17, 2013, in a bit of a funk because all I could think about was me not being able to walk with my class across that stage to receive my diploma, especially with my cousins and the few other people I started out with. I called the graduate sales people later that day to see if I could get my money back for the cap and gown that was still at the school, so they told me they'll send me a check in the mail since I didn't get a chance to use it. I spent that day with just a moment to myself to recap everything I had been through and had taken place in my life at that time in order to try to piece some things together but got nothing from it.

Things had slowly started to seem like it was falling apart in my world, and I didn't know how to react to something such as that. I would black out and freeze up, and when people would call my name or say something to me, I'd just give them this blank stare before even answering. I went through a bit of depression because I knew I wasn't going to be able to get that chance to walk again or be able to have that feeling of knowing what it was like that I could someday tell my kids and I could feel proud about it.

I spent the whole weekend feeling sorry for myself while others were out celebrating their big accomplishments. I was done with school; I just didn't have the diploma to show for it at that time. A part of me felt defeated and damaged by all that I had done because, in the end, it wasn't enough. I thought it was karma hitting me back tenfold for some of the things that I done or said to others in the past. I didn't even get on social media that whole weekend because I knew I was going to see grad pictures from everyone else all over Facebook and Instagram.

Being depressed, I then went into a bit of rage where I wanted revenge, but I knew it wouldn't solve anything. I felt angry at everyone because that would've been my time to shine, but instead, I was at home in my bed, feeling bad because I didn't make it.

After about a week, when things had started to settle down, it didn't bother me as much because I knew there was nothing I could do about it but to just move on from it. I had this fuck it mind-set about everything and everybody during that time. I couldn't go back and rewind the hands of time to prevent that to happen to me. I just asked the Lord to give me strength because I still have this feeling that I can still make it till the end. I then got a text that week later from my counselor, suggesting that I take more E2020 test prep in order to prepare myself so that I could pass the test over the summer. I didn't want to at first because it wouldn't have been the same because graduation had already passed and everything was just a blur to me and I felt like it would've all been for nothing.

After having some time to think about it and clear my head, I then decided I would go forth with the online class to help prepare me for the test again and see where it would take me. Truth be told, I didn't really have it in me do it anymore because I was so burned out from doing all that work I did the summer before that. I wanted no part in it anymore, like looking at that computer screen, which is probably the reason why I didn't do so well academically on that test in the first place. I continued with the prep work, but only that time, I didn't spend so much time on doing it sporadically.

A part of me thought that maybe I put so much pressure on myself when I was taking those online courses to the point that, when it came time to take the actual test, I would crash and burn and forget everything that I had learned. I didn't have to sit through actual summer school class like the other seniors that didn't get to walk, but I did come and sit through the little tutoring session a couple days before the test even started. You could say I was the lucky one to not have to deal with that headache because it was already hot in the classrooms.

As the time came for me to take the test again, I felt a little anxious and nervous, but surprisingly, I didn't let it bother me like it normally would. By that time, I was over the whole situation as to how I got played and took the test. Whatever would happen at that point would happen, and there was nothing more I could possibly do about it. I had that it-is-what-it-is attitude from then on out. I had prayed on it and put it all in God's hands because, at that moment, I knew I was going to pass it that time around, but if I didn't, I wouldn't have let it phase me as much as it should because what I was hoping and praying for was out the window from that point on. It's like a numb feeling that rushed over my shoulders without a care in the world. Had I not passed that test, I probably would've just left school and done something else with my time.

After taking the test, I left the school just as confident as I ever was from knowing that I passed that time around because I didn't put so much pressure on myself. A couple days later, I texted the school's secretary to see if I had actually passed the test that time around or if I would have to take the geometry part the next week later. She responded with a quickness, leaving my heart beating fast, excited on opening the text to see what she had said. As I unlocked my phone and opened the text to see that she said I passed the test with flying colors. I scored above what I had hoped for, leaving me completely speechless and a big relief off of my shoulders. Words couldn't explain how happy I felt because I had been battling for the longest time, trying to pass that test, and I actually did. I had score in the eighties range that time, which threw me over what I would normally make on tests, which would be in the sixties, almost seventies, range. I was just so happy that my war was finally over and I could finally put all that behind me from that point.

I still felt bad as to how things played out with my situation, but I didn't let that stop me from doing what I was set out to do. I went back to school for about a week or two to get my diploma. I have been relieved from stress and still have this faith that I will start my new journey and a new chapter of my life. Back then, I didn't understand why I went through what I did, but looking back at it now, I'm very much thankful because he knew what was best for me in that situation, so I took that and ran with it from there on. I didn't let that break me, and I'm so grateful I went through what I did to this day because it made me so much stronger. Now that that part of my situation was taken care of, I then finished focusing on getting into school at the University as a business major.

    I had already got accepted from when I first applied back in March earlier that year. My ACT scores weren't as high as they should've been although they were almost there. I still had to take the compass test in order to be fully accepted into University that was something else added onto the frustration I already had. After walking around the campus that whole day trying to find the room, I was scheduled to take the test and finally came across to someone sitting in the room while taking the computer exam. I was the only one in there to take the test, which left me to assume everybody had already taken theirs because I was having a difficult time finding the class. I exceeded on both the English and math portions of the test, but what really pushed me to the top was my English score on the test. The English part of the test consisted mostly of reading comprehension and constructed response questions with a few multiple choices as well. After getting my scores back that same day, I then faxed my scores later that day to make sure I got into school on time so that I could get my classes put in.

    After having such a big setback in my life a few months prior to that, that let me knew that I needed to buckle down a bit more and stay on top of my stuff from then on.

9
College Life Rolls Around

Early registration started, and I had to be at the school early that morning to get my alternate pin for my classes so that I could be fully registered and have my stuff situated, which was a hassle for both my cousins, who helped me get in school my first year there. I had to go put my classes in and map out my schedule to how I wanted it, but it didn't turn out how I had planned because I had class every day of the week. I lucky to have had only one on that Friday and the man wasn't even a hard class to begin with. I then got fully situated and started my new journey on the right path, although I must admit, I hit a few bumps in the road because I didn't have enough financial aid to cover my books the week before classes even started when I went to the bookstore to go purchase them. That predicament by itself caused me to have to go get back in that ass financial aid line with the rest of the students to see if they could up my student loans so that everything would be taken care of in time before classes started the following week for my books, meal plan, etc.

This was my first year in college, so I started as an independent student which made it a little more complicated for me. Once all of that was settled, I then proceeded on a good route by going to class every day until I started slacking just like any other typical college student. Some days, I woke up and just feel didn't like going to class, so I stayed in bed on days I didn't want to get up and be bothered with anyone. My roommate was barely there because he had his own car; plus, he talked to this girl on campus and went home, like every weekend, but we were cool. The only issue that I had with him was that he wasn't the cleanest person, and I had to tell him that he needed to clean his side of the room, especially if he was going to bring somebody in there because that wasn't a good look on both of us.

I started out having pretty good grades throughout the first year of taking the courses, but things started to take a turn for me at the end of my first semester when one of my teachers in the English department gave me a whole zero at the end of the semester because he suspected that I plagiarized my paper, which I could honestly say that I didn't. The topic was just so difficult, I had to research a lot of the material I put into my paper so that I could make sure that I knew what I was talking about and be able to back it up if he decided to ask me something about it. I think what really made him give me a zero was because I didn't include a works cited page at the end of my paper, making me having to retake my whole English class all over again for the upcoming spring semester. The rest of my grades were quite good for my first semester there so that was a plus, and I didn't let that F get me down.

When we came back from Christmas break, I enrolled in his English 102 class with my cousin and told myself I'd worry about English 101 the next semester after that. When class was getting ready to start, he pulled out in the hall and told me that I needed to drop his class because of that zero he gave me the last semester and go enroll back in the first one.

One of my friends on campus told me that there's a lady teacher who taught a very easy lesson, so I immediately went to her office to get an override. Luckily, she was so kind enough to let me at that time since she had already reached the capacity of students. Looking back from where I was before to where I'm at now, molded me into a young man I am today, considering how long it took me to get to the finish line. The journey helped me get through a lot of tough times in my life, and I can't even front. It also felt like I was putting up a war there from trying my hardest to finish even when the stakes where so high.

During the process of getting that English class situated, I then faced another problem in one of my classes with another one of my professors in that same semester. That one actually tried everything in his power to bring me down and I had absolute pure hell the whole month I stayed in his class before actually considering dropping him. I failed the first test he gave us, which was a no brainer because of the type of work he had us doing. Some of us didn't understand the work at all, but the majority did, and he made it seemed as if we were slow, so me being the person that I was, I went to his office and told him I didn't understand any of his work and that I failed the first test that he gave us. He didn't know who I was because he was one of those teachers that you had to interact with in order for him to know who you were, and plus, he showed favoritism to the students he liked the most.

When I went to him as a concerned student about my grade, he basically insinuated that I should drop his class with no hesitation, but he only told me in so many words. I caught on to what he was saying, but at the same time, I was trying to make it work because I didn't want to give up just that easy. He had some students in the class that were straight A students who he knew personally and who would literally kiss this man's ass just to get what they wanted from him, even if it meant sabotaging someone else to get what they wanted, and I saw that with people in business and marketing department which is why I excluded myself from that situation. When I went back to meet with him that second time around for another meeting about me and the few other students who were having trouble in his class. He then told me I wasn't gone make anything out of myself but call himself trying to say it in a way to make it sound less rude but it really wasn't any other way he could've phrased that. At that moment, I felt disrespected not only as a student but as a person as well. One of the teachers in the department overheard him, so the teacher and any other concerned professor took preliminary action against his behavior. I was just going to let it go at first because I didn't want to cost the man his job because of something that he said to me, but she was persistent about taking some action against that kind of behavior. We went to the head of the department to take some serious action once he said that because, not only did he discourage me, but the others who were in the same situation as I was, were scared or didn't want to say anything.

After taking some action against what he said to me, it didn't really solve anything about that matter. I don't even know what they said to him when I stepped out, but I do know that they had some words with him for telling me something like that. So after I got out of his class in relief, I then signed to another professor, who was teaching the same class that semester. I get in the other man's class, and he's going over a few chapters with everyone that I already knew what to expect from him.

When the class ended, our teacher mentioned that our first examination will be in our next meeting. I stared at him sharply because we're just in the middle of the semester and now he's already giving us an exam. I just joined the class and I have no idea what I need to study. I didn't know any of the material that they had went over in the class because I transferred into his class in the middle of the semester, which was around the month of February at that time I knew a few people from other classes but we were not cool as them, they seemed to look like they are not listening because everyone is busy on their phones while the teacher is lecturing.

Once class was over, I then proceeded toward him, asking about the test and could I have an extension since it was only my first day in his class. He told me, "No." That just because I was new to the class didn't mean a thing because I was transferring to his and that he didn't have a lot of time because he had a certain time where he had to have everybody's test graded and in the system. I then proceeded to my dorm to cram those four chapters of the book they went over in class that I missed out on so that I could possibly have an understanding of what to expect when it came time to take the test.

That following Thursday came, and as I reached for the test, my mind was all over the place because I hardly knew anything that was on it. Leaving the class, I just knew I bombed the hell out of that test because I was new in the class and I was expected to take the test as soon as I entered the man's class and be able to pass it all at once, which had me overwhelmed.

People always tell me to stop being so negative, but I was never being negative. It's just that I knew what the outcome was going to be, and I was honestly was okay with that. Sometimes you just have that gut feeling about a lot of things, and most of the time, I'd be spot on about whatever it was that I was feeling at the moment. It seemed like I would always be right about every obstacle that I had to endure in my life, and I must say, my intuition was next level which is why I still trust my instincts to this day. Half the people wouldn't understand; they'd just think I was being, like I said, negative, or just trying to bring them down, which was far from the case because I never said anything negative about them. They'd ask, and I would imply with the answer that I was already thinking in the first place. I never really had anyone in my corner after my mama died three years ago besides my uncle and my cousin, but the rest would usually throw it in my face that mama handicapped me or hindered me from a lot of things in life today since she's been gone.

Cut to the next week, we got our test scores back from that following week, and when I saw my grade, it wasn't even a shock to me that I failed the test. With me being the concerned student that I was, I then wanted to talk with my professor about my grade and try to see if I could do anything to bring my grade up, especially since I had just got into the man's class and I didn't want to repeat how I was in that other class. While talking to him, he told me he doesn't give extra credit work and that I should probably drop his class as well. I then started to think that me attending college was a joke and that maybe I should just give up since I was just starting out at the time.

After telling me that, I then went to go see my advisor to get a drop slip, but I didn't want to because he would try with every breath in him to persuade me to stay in the class, knowing I was failing in the first place. I didn't want to talk to him because I had already had a run in with him about the same class I was in before that about dropping it. He then tried to persuade me to stay in the class before giving me the drop slip, but I didn't want to hear anything he had to say to me in that moment because, if I'm failing the class and the professor telling me to drop the course, then why would I stay, knowing that I'm going to fail it in the first place. That would hurt me in the long run. I'm looking at this man like, "Why the hell would I stay in this class if I'm failing it?" That grade won't look good on my transcript in the near future when I apply for jobs later on in life.

After he didn't give me my drop slip the last that time around, I then went to a much friendlier advisor next door to him. He wasn't foreign like the majority of them in that department and was easy to talk to as well, unlike the other ones that had to be so difficult. I then told him I needed to drop one of my classes, and he instantly gave me a drop slip without any hesitation or a lecture behind it. He could actually see why I needed to drop the course in the first place, once I told him my reason. We had a quick conversation as I walked toward the door leaving his office and that was it. He told me that he understood and I got to do what I got to do in order to help myself. I proceeded out his office to take my drop slip to the register's office and dropped the class.

My financial aid advisor said it wouldn't mess up my grade because I still had a pretty good GPA that last semester, despite that F I had in my English class. I wasn't considered a full-time student anymore, but I didn't care at that moment. I just felt a sense of relief and like a big weight had been lifted off my shoulders. I was just glad that I rid myself of that headache from that class and all the trouble that came along with it and those difficult professors.

My cousin, on the other hand, dropped one of her chemistry classes as I dropped my computer systems class because she too had a difficult professor. It then went through our heads to change our majors, but we didn't change them within that point because we still wanted to give our majors that we were already in another shot. I ended that semester off with an overall good GPA, and I had the dean's list once I dropped that computer class.

Throughout the summer, I had to focus on trying to become an independent student so that I could get more money for the next school year, since my first year didn't go how it should've gone when it came to all my student loans. So that following summer, I had to go through the process of getting my biological mama's birth certificate and my dad's as well along with a bunch of other information that I couldn't get because the files for my dad's was lost a long time ago back in 94. My grandma had my mama's information put up into a little safety box with a key she kept put up, just in case she had to go in it. I had trouble looking for my daddy's information because no one knew where it could be found, but somehow, after trying my hardest to get his information, God came through for me, and my stuff got waived, and I became an independent student that following semester without any of his information in my school files all because I had my mama's.

10

The Rock of Our Family's Death

The following school year came, and I was still a struggling business major, but I somehow pushed through it because I wasn't taking the same teachers anymore. I knew I'd cross paths again with the professors I had to drop that spring semester, so then I started thinking of ways that I wouldn't have to look at them again which would've been impossible, due to the fact they were the only two teaching certain classes. I didn't really have a problem with one of them, just the one who discouraged me. With my grandma going back and forth out of the hospital, I stayed with her on days I didn't have classes because she didn't want to stay in the hospital by herself, and I would do anything for her just because she was like my actual mama that she bent over backwards for me the most.

Things then started to take a turn for the worst because I could literally see her health was declining fast, and she wasn't as jolly as she used to be. Some days, she would have hand on her head like she was tired of being here, because we had lost so many loved ones in the process, not to mention another death we faced around the month of April who was another grandchild she had raised, that she had to bury as well. They would always say that she had these picks and chooses of who could get anything out of her besides just me, and the two that she lost before her passing were the next ones that could. You could tell my grandmother was barely hanging on by a limb and she was trying to keep pushing like the strong woman we knew she was. Every time we took pictures together, you could see in her face that she was slowly going down. She got to the point of where she'd often say, I'm

Life's Scars and Wisdom

just so tired and ready to go home. Me being the person that I was, I didn't want to hear her talk the way that she did because it would hurt me that she was hurting and I couldn't do anything but sit there and look so helpless. I wished I could've taken the pain that she was feeling and lord knows I would have, then I thought, Okay, she just talking because she's going to be around for a very long time to come.

We don't often pay attention to the signs that God is trying to show us at that moment because we're so caught up in something else or just blind to the fact of what he was trying to reveal to our family, not knowing that he may be given us signals or he's trying to tell us something that we are unaware of.

At that point, I'm thinking that we were going to pass all of that because, when you see your loved one going through it, you don't know exactly what to feel, especially when it's your mama of all people just lying on a hospital bed.

As the semester goes by, I then got a letter from the RA in our building telling me that I had to move over to another room we come back from Christmas break. I didn't have a roommate anymore and it's not a big problem at all. I called my mama the next day to check on her because we had this big disagreement about something that I must admit I was wrong, but I didn't think about stuff like that back then. So she asked me whether I am coming home, because she's looking forward that I will come home every weekend since I was twenty-five minutes away from home. I told her no because she'd pissed me off about that one little thing.

After we got off the phone, I didn't call her for about five days, which seemed like a week to me because I don't normally go that long without talking to my mama.

After not hearing from her a few days later, I then put my pride to the side and called her to see how she was doing and making sure she was in good spirits She then gave me the news that she would be going back into the hospital again, and when I tell y'all that I almost fell out because I don't like my mama being sick, especially when I don't know about it! I asked her why this time because she'd been in and out of the hospital that whole fall semester I was in school and that summer as well. She said it's the same old problem with her legs giving her trouble because they had started swollen up. She was light-skinned, so her legs would swell up and become big and red, so I was like, "Okay, I'll be staying with you whenever I'm done taking the final exam and after I moved to my next room." The class was ready to take the final exam and it was kind of difficult for me since I don't know exactly the subject. I immediately rushed out of the class without checking the back of my test and failed the course all because of a mistake I had made, but my mama was more important to me at the time, so I didn't care about any of that.

When she first went into the hospital, everyone thought she would be in there for about a week or week in a half and they would finally release her right before Christmas. Little did we know, she ended up staying just about a whole month in there, all just for her legs, which had all of us puzzled at the same time because we didn't think it was going to be that serious.

She went from a regular room to the ICU, and I must say that when we heard the news, it had my whole family in shock and disbelief at that time because we didn't know what to expect. Everyone started to put things into perspective at that time because we thought we were going to lose her then, so everyone started to come together and huddle around her, but it was like a false alarm. I think he was preparing us then to get ready for what was about to happen next.

We were coming back and forth like every single day to see her in order to make sure that she was alright because, at the time, we were all a divided family, but I could see more of a division between us when she got her wings and left us. She kept us more together compared to what we are now because everyone would all meet up at her house for family gatherings or to just sit around, laugh, and have a good time.

We thought she would've been able to come home before the holidays, but unfortunately, she ended up spending Christmas in the hospital, which was her birthday as well, but that didn't stop us from celebrating her big day without her. To show how much we loved and appreciated her, everyone showed up, bearing gifts, for her on her 81st birthday like we were doing throughout the month in order to make sure that her day was just as special like any other year.

I didn't stay with her when they put her back in a regular room because there are a lot of things going on at the time and nobody could stay with her. They wanted to keep her monitored to make sure she was doing alright. About a day or two later, my aunt and I stayed in the hospital before they discharged her and sent her home. The day before New Year's Eve, they told us that she will be released and ready to go home by New Year's Day, which was a relief because I had missed my mama being at the house with me every day, because things just wasn't the same. She wasn't really able to move when they got her out the bed because she had been in a hospital about a month and not being able to get up and do for herself like she normally could around the house, made her lose the little strength she had to regain.

The day right before she got out, everyone wanted me to stay that one last night with her, but I wasn't really feeling it because I didn't like sleeping on those pull-out chairs because I couldn't sleep at night, so I went home even though she really wanted me to stay that last night in there with her. They say that as you get older, you think things through more, and if I knew then what I know now, I would've stay with my mama that night in the hospital. Now, about three, almost four, years later, it hurt me that I didn't, and it bothers me from time to time whenever I think about it. Grieving is truly a process and I've accepted mines to the fullest extent that I can.

That following morning after New Year's, the doctors were getting ready to discharge her and send her home. My uncle and brother was headed back out to get her that following morning, not knowing that the ambulance was already on their way with her. They bought her home that morning and got her into bed with ease although she was yelling at some of them because she thought they were going to drop her on the floor. We were right there by her side whenever she needed anything because she couldn't do nothing at the time being, not even feed herself.

She hated for anybody to clean her because she didn't want to feel as if she was being a burden to anyone, which was not even the case. That was just what she thought because she was so used to being independent and doing things on her own. She slept the whole day after we fed her some home-cooked food since she didn't really eat any hospital foods because it lacks seasoning and just didn't taste right. I felt so helpless and somewhat bad about her situation because I knew she was uncomfortable to have all of us standing around her. I lend her a helping hand because she couldn't really do anything for herself. She's been lying in the hospital without someone to have her up to move around.

With school getting ready to start back, I didn't know whether I wanted to go back or not with Mama not being able to help herself; plus, I didn't want to meet my new roommate because the room I walked in before we got out was nasty, but I didn't let that stop me from focusing on my mama at that point in time. School was the last thing on my mind, but I went back because that's where she wanted me to be, and I would do anything to make her happy and keep that smile on her face.

The rest of the family tended to her every need because we knew she wasn't going to ask anybody to do anything for her to quick. A little after the spring semester started, I would always come home that exact Thursday evening after I finished classes to check on my mama and be there for her just like everybody else since I didn't have class on Fridays.

After a couple weeks had flown by, she then slowly started to regain her strength and sitting up on her own like she normally was. When I walked through the door, I seen her sitting up in her wheelchair, moving around, and I just knew in the back of my mind that things were getting ready to get back to normal around the house, but that still wasn't the case that following Sunday morning. She had a memory loss for a few seconds that left both me and my brother looking confused as because she called me a different name. That hadn't happened in years since her sugar went down a time before then. It's like her mind went blank for a few seconds, and then it snapped back once I asked her how many fingers I was holding up. In the back of my mind, I knew something just wasn't right with that situation, but I left it alone because I was young and didn't think that much about all of that back then like I do now. I then went out and stayed gone that whole day, driving with one of my cousins who were teaching me how to drive because I was late in learning.

We were gone for at 4 or 5 hours, making sure I had everything packed down and knew what to do while being in heavy traffic. When I got back, she was still in bed sound asleep like she had never awaken earlier. My cousins and aunts came in later that night to check on her in order to see how she was doing at the moment. They said she hadn't woken up since I had left the house earlier that day. I went into the kitchen to fix myself something to eat, and a thought occurred to me that mama hadn't eaten at all that day, but I was like I'd just feed her when she wakes up because she was sleeping so peacefully, I didn't want to disturb her, so I just let her slept. A part of me was feeling bad that I missed the wide-awake, alert Mama that I once had that would be up laughing and cursing us out if something wasn't done a particular way, she wanted it to be. I guess when she's in the hospital, all she had to do was lying in bed, sleeping all day and that's what she's used to during that time. That situation really made me trust my gut feeling because it seemed like it never stirred me wrong, which is why I have so many negative outlooks on life today. She then woke up and was in good spirits, interacting with everybody like nothing was wrong.

We were getting ready to give her a bath and clean her up before the night was over because we knew she hadn't had one that whole weekend and then feed her as well because we knew she had been in the bed all day sleeping and hadn't eaten yet. We started laughing and joking around about other things, and she started talking to us about her past mistakes, which was surprising to me because that was the first time she shared something that I never heard before. Now, my grandma had nine kids, and we all knew she had a miscarriage, but we didn't know she also had an abortion or anything of that matter, so it kind of took us all by surprise. Her exact words while lying in that bed were, "I had an abortion, and that's something that I'm not proud of." And right along with that, she then said that she asked the Lord to forgive her because that's something that she was holding onto her whole life. It's like she knew she was getting ready to leave us, and something didn't set right with me when she said it, but typical me was shocked, but I then brushed it off like I would normally do. She told us that one of my twin cousins was pregnant and trying to hide it from her, which was the reason why she brought up the story about abortion in the first place. She couldn't say anything, which was crazy at the time because my cousin thought that she didn't know, but you can't hide anything from older people because they knew everything. She told our grandma that she was about to get an abortion, but she told her don't make that same mistake I made.

After Mama was done saying what she had to say, it left us shook that she actually admitted something like that after all these years because that was something that we never would've fathomed. It's like she knew for the longest that she was getting ready to leave us but didn't say anything to us. In fact, another one of my cousins said that it seemed like she was getting ready to breathe it out to her at one point in time while she was in the hospital but didn't want to say it because she didn't know how any of us was going to react to hearing something of that sort. While we were getting ready to clean her up, I then went into my room for a second to check my phone and get on Instagram and Snapchat to see what was happening at the time. I then heard one of my cousins say, "Maw maw, wake up. Her eyes going to the back of her head!"

I immediately stormed back into the room when I heard her say that because I had a feeling something was getting ready to happen. We got the fan to try and cool her down, but that didn't seem to work. She was steady fading in and out, trying her best to stay with us, but we couldn't reach her, so we went to go get the rest of my aunts and called the town ambulance, but they weren't in town and it took them the longest to arrive. I went outside to clear my head while we waited for their arrival.

While pacing back and forth as the tears started pouring down my face thinking, "Is this really happening right now?"

I then hear one of my aunts crying in the background because we couldn't believe what was happening right before our very eyes. I then hit the mailbox so hard in a rage of frustration and anger that it was actually taking the ambulance so long.

After waiting about forty-five minutes, the ambulance finally arrived at the house, which was already too late to begin with because my brother and uncle already tried to perform CPR on her to begin with. As soon as the ambulance got out, my cousin and I approached

Life's Scars and Wisdom

the ambulance and asked them why it took so long when there's a patient who urgently needs their help. Our aunt tried to calm us down before I panicked and zoned out completely.

They immediately rushed into the house, laying my mama on the cold surface of the floor in the hallway and hooking her up to a breathing machine. Something told me that my mama was already dead because she hated to be cold, and I knew, once they put her on that cold floor and she didn't say anything that she was gone from our lives forever. As I sat there so helplessly as usual, watching the people try to save my mama's life, I knew it was already too late for that. I just knew my mama was gone and that my dream had actual turned into a reality, not only for me but for my whole family with a look of devastations. I had always dreams about losing her, but I always knew it was a dream until that exact night when it finally happened. I'm worried that my worst dream will become a reality. I think God is preparing me that day to accept that fear and the fact that everything happens for a reason. I just had to be ready for what was to come next even though I felt as if my whole life flashed right before my very eyes. I just didn't think it would've happened so soon and that I would've experienced something so heart-wrenching with my heart beating fast to where it felt as if though I couldn't breathe or hardly move. As everyone on our street, including others from across the town, crowded around the house, we then waited for the ambulance to come out of the house in order to tell us what was going on although we pretty much already knew because she had stopped breathing way before they even came. You would've thought it was another crime scene with the way everyone was scattered around our house, trying to see what was going on, especially that late at night. Some people were just so nosey; they can't help not to mind their own business and tend to what they were doing, but that's pretty much how it is in this small town. As the ambulance came out, we followed them to the emergency room uptown to see if they could possibly bring her back to us. We all waited in the waiting room with everyone having this puzzled look on their faces as to what was going to happen next.

The nurse came in with this sad facial expression, and I just knew what he was about to say as he told all of us to come into the waiting room. His exacts words were, "I'm so sorry, but unfortunately, she didn't make it, but I will let you all have a moment to come in and say your goodbyes."

Everyone burst out and scream with tears running on their faces when we heard the tragic news. We didn't expect it but we already knew that it will happen. I was in a shock at that moment, so I didn't know what to think or how to react to a situation such as that, but it seemed like my dream had finally come true in that exact same setting just like a déjà vu feeling. I felt so depressed, pissed off, and mix of emotions during that moment because I wasn't prepared for that to happen. I sat back and hoping that this was all a dream. I stayed with my cousin that night, who'd been there with me since we were kids. I couldn't even think straight or even walk a straight line at that time because no one knew that we'd lose our backbone so soon. I thought I was going to faint for a second or two because it seemed so unreal to hear news like that, especially around that time of night. It seemed like my whole world tumbling down and my life became a mess after she passed away. My phone was constantly ringing left and right from people calling and texting me trying to check and see how I was doing. I was mad at God for taking someone so precious that was near and dear to me, but I knew I had to turn to the him because, the way I was feeling, I had thought about killing myself just to take myself out of my misery. I felt like nobody understood the pain I was going through, or that they even cared for me, which was okay because I can pick my own self back up. And it still feels like that to this very day I often tend to not express how I feel about it. I don't really like people feeling sorry for me just by trying to get their attention, nor do I want a pity party from anyone.

Right after all of that took place, I stayed up the highway with my cousin and auntie that night after her passing, which was kind of ironic because I had never been up the highway to see their place before. We stayed up half the night with conversations about her with my phone constantly going off sporadically with "I'm so sorry for your loss" texts and phone calls, putting me deeper in my feelings. I laid there on the couch with tears pouring down my face and not an ounce of understanding. I woke up that next morning, hoping it was all a dream, but as I got up, it hit me that reality just hit me in my face, and it was time for me to step up. I questioned God's work so many times, especially throughout that night since it was so fresh to me and also many other nights after that in particular because of how it hit all of us at once and no one expected it. We all tend to go through things in life that we are often not prepared for and I must say, that really hit home for me. I never felt that type of pain before, nor did I think that would happen so soon in my life at just the age of twenty years old. With me not knowing my real biological parents to having the next closest ones in my life taken away at a split instant.

I tossed and turned many nights, not really knowing what to expect. I really just wanted my life to be over at that point, but I had to keep pushing because I knew nothing was going to happen to me anytime soon. The saying, "You never miss a good thing until it's gone" is a true statement, and I had to learn that the hard way in order to have peace on some things. This lesson actually humbled me a bit more compared to how I used to be, and I have to say it gets better daily. Her words often come back to bite me in my ass today.

She would always to say, "Y'all gone miss me when I'm gone, just watch and see," especially with a bunch of other stuff I got going on in my everyday life that I couldn't even explain or talk about with anyone else but her. I miss our talks that we used to have over the phone from me leaving class, going into my dorm room and talking about some of everything from her asking me how my day went.

It's the small things that matters the most and you never take for granted because one day it's here and the next, it's gone. I could really use her guidance and comfort at the moment, but a part of me knows that I'm never going to get that back in my life, so now I just march to my own beat without needing anybody's, including my so-called family's, validation of me and what they thought of me all these years. All the good times and laughter we shared in her living room to the front porch as a family is a thing of the past now.

She basically was what held our family together in the first place. Now everybody barely talks or checks upon one another unless they're trying to be nosey, which is a sad case if you ask me, but you actually find out who's really there for you when it all boils down and those who just want to give their opinion on something, they knew nothing about. Everyone secretly talks bad about one another behind each other's back and it don't even have to be like, but I believe it's either jealously or envy. You have those that will voice their opinion of you but won't do a damn thing for you but criticize you just to get a reaction, and others will side with them as well just because of what they do for one another. It seems like certain cliques were formed, which I am absolutely no part of it.

The day of her funeral finally came, and I honestly could not believe we were getting ready to bury the only mother I have ever known anything about since I was a two-month-old baby. It's odd because, when the funeral got ready to start, one of my aunts, who was her firstborn and looked the most like her, sat in the same spot where she'd normally sit at whenever we had a funeral for someone in the family we had lost years before that. I was alright when the funeral first started although I didn't want anybody touching me, telling me the usual, "Everything's going to be alright" or "She's in a better place," like they normally do because, at that point in time, I felt like it wasn't going to be, and people just tend to tell you that either because they don't know what else to say. But I rather a person not say anything to me at that point because my response might not be what they want to hear of the way I'm feeling at that moment.

To this day, when someone loses a parent or just a loved one in general, I never approach them because I never know how they're feeling, and that there's really nothing that I could possibly say because it's a hard pill to swallow, not just for me but for anybody.

A lot of people cope with things differently, and let's just say that when I lost her, I was all over the place. I've told plenty of people that approached me back then and said the same thing to me because that's not going to bring that person that you loved so deeply, back, so now I take that with me as grain of salt and go on about my day.

I hate the way that my life played out in all of this because, sometimes, I feel as if I have nobody in this world with me that understands my situation. While the funeral was going on, they started playing the song, "Troubles Don't Last Always," and tears instantly started to fall down my face like no other. I got light-headed as they lifted up my

Life's Scars and Wisdom

mama's casket for us all to walk up and view her body one last time before taking her to the grave site and putting her into the ground.

I felt so empty at the thought of knowing I'd never see her again in life, so I had to ask myself, "Am I really dreaming this whole day?"

It's amazing how she played such a big impact in not only my life but my family's and whoever else she came across as a whole because, ever since she left God's green earth, things just haven't been the same, nor will it ever be again. If I sat here and told y'all all of this was fake, then I'd be lying to the whole world although sometimes I wish it was a made-up fantasy so I could hide behind the ugly truth that have stumbled upon my family and I.

I wish it was all a dream; that way, the pain I've been feeling for the past three years could just go away, but sadly, life doesn't always work in our favor that way. Sometimes I felt like I was in denial to some of the things I was exposed to because no one ever told me it would be this way. After all of that took place, I could honestly say I didn't want to be there with any of my family members after she passed away. The backlash I would receive from a lot of them, left me in a funny place on how I view them. I mean of course we still talk, but it's not like it used to be. It's still so very hard for me to get myself together without her presence at times, but I'm slowly finding my way that they said I couldn't. I haven't heard her voice for so long, I thought I'm going crazy after all that happened, and I hope that I will overcome this in the end because I've accomplished so much in my life and I try to keep pushing to become better.

It seemed like once she passed away, every elderly on our street started to pass away as well in the same exact month or a little after that. We had about three deaths in our family within the first five months of that year right along with a neighbor we had known for years and a school teacher who taught some of my family members, like my cousins and brother. She even kept all of us out of trouble here and there when we were kids and would cover up for us when it all came down to it.

To be honest, during that time, I didn't know whether I was going or coming for that matter because I was still in such a shock about my mama's passing, which made me want to try to stand on my own two feet and just be able to grow from my life's experiences because it left me with this story to tell as my testimony. I walked around with this chip on my shoulders and how I viewed people because of what happened with my situation.

I was always told that my mama hindered me from a lot of things by my family members, and it seem like every little thing that came out of some of their mouths were negative or a snarky remark, just because she had me a certain kind of way from the rest of them. Even now, someone will mention it or bring it up in some type of way. I guess trying to make me feel some type of way about myself whether it's an argument or something else that breaks out.

Three months later, I turned 21 and was finally legal and old enough to go to the boat and see what it was like to finally gamble because I had never really got into the hype until then. I never went till later that year because I was so crashed out that day about it being very first birthday without mama, but the friends I had then were able to keep her off my mind for a bit. I didn't know what to feel, so I just went out to eat with some friends and later came back and went to a kickback where this one girl was making mixed drinks. Normally, I don't drink around people because you never know what they are capable of, but I made an exception that day. I did watch my intake because you never know what would happen on that campus when somebody gets drunk, and people take advantage of you.

11

My Very First Job

A month later right after school was out, I got my very first job working at McDonald's. There I was either placed on the grill or working the table, fixing the food. I hated working on the tables because rush hour would come and the screen would fill up with tons of orders. But with the help of my other coworkers, we got the job done.

After my first week of training, they literally cut my hours to where I only had about seven–eight hours that week, which was literally only one day of the week. I immediately went on Indeed jobs and applied for other jobs but had no luck at the time because they either weren't hiring, or at least that's what they'd tell me and I didn't quite understand the position of some of them. As time progressed, my hours picked back up, but school started back, and I couldn't work on certain days they wanted me to come in due to me being in class all day. It didn't matter to me at that time because I was over working at that place because of the people and their attitudes, especially with the rude owner who stopped by two or three times out of the week just to criticize how we make the food when he didn't always do it right himself. He even sent me home one day for not having on a belt, but the small amount of weight that I had on me, kept the pants up. I went through so much throughout the year of 2015 that I didn't stop to think about how much I had on my plate and how it was affecting me mentally all at once.

Before school started back, my family had this intervention for me and how they think I'm going crazy and losing my mind. I'm nowhere near their presence, but my name gets brought up a lot on how they think I'm this or how they think I'm that. I guess because of my behavior or what they thought, but my thing is, don't just look at my attitude on things, they should've looked at theirs because they don't have some of the best attitudes either. It was a little hurtful to know that's how they really felt about me, I kept it pushing. It's one thing to tell a person about themselves, but for me, if you see me going down the wrong path, don't just throw criticism at my face and not offer a helping hand. I still see it to this very day although I tend to look over it a whole lot better than what I used to.

As school started, I began my first semester off campus and commuted from home every day. I wanted a new car badly but knew I couldn't afford one at the time because I was only working McDonald's, which gave a minimum-wage salary and I barely had the hours. I continued to drive my uncle's car that he had purchased about a week or two before school even started. I drove his car every day until I got my refund where he then helped me purchase the car, so that I could have a way back and forth. We bought the car from one of my other cousins, who stayed in Dallas since she was trying to find another one.

Throughout the school year, we got a new unexpected professor who came into our department, who stayed giving tests like every week. I had straight Fs from her tests and just couldn't get with it for some reason, but I wasn't the only one. In the back of my mind, I'm like, "I'm not going to pass this class." That lady was new and too strict for any of us to be able to handle. She wouldn't even give the majority of the class, who needed take-home work to bring up their grade by the end of the semester; that's just how strict and unreasonable she was. Later that semester, she put us into groups where we had to present our presentations to the class. I'm thinking that was a sure sign of us maybe passing the class if we do well on her presentation. Little did I know, she averaged the rest of our grades from our test with the presentations, and the majority of the class ended up failing her class and having to retake her again. But I wasn't one of those people.

My cousin passed her class, but I ended up with a D in that course at the end. That led me to believe that she was going graduate and leave me behind because the classes I had a hard time in, she easily got through them even if she barely made it out. We had this goal that we were going to graduate and come out together after we both switched our majors to the same. Even when we had different majors, we said we were going to graduate together.

After failing the course, I told myself I would never take that lady for anything else again throughout the rest of my college courses, and I did just that in the end. Every time I went to register for my classes and I see her name on the list, I'd scroll past her name and chose another instructor. If she was the only one teaching the course at the time, I literally would wait until they added another one. The department didn't have many teachers to choose from, but the few we had weren't so bad.

During that semester, my grades weren't the best, but I was passing, so it didn't really matter to me. Most of my grades around that time were mostly Cs with a B or two here and there but no As at all. I struggled to try and get an A, but it just wasn't possible, considering the fact that nobody in the class hardly like to read about the stuff that we took a test on. We had to read about two or three chapters with one chapter being about forty pages long itself. Every time I tried to crack open a book to read, I'm ready to close it and go to sleep after about five pages into the chapter. She lectured to the majority of us that if we took the time out to read the book and not just purchase it, we would actually pass the tests that she was giving us.

To me, it wouldn't have worked if we read it anyway because the chapters were so long, by the time you get to the next chapter, you already done forgot what you read in the last chapter and I wasn't big on taking notes while reading anyway. I was not the world's best test taker but I continued my way through, even on days where I felt like the odds was stacked against me and had absolutely nothing to show for it. I began to hate going to class because I started to feel like it was just a waste of my time and that I would never get out at the rate we were going.

You could say this stuff was breaking me mentally as well, and I felt so lost and confused at that time, like it was a cry out for help, but no one could hear me. I thought I was just here living and that was it because no excitement was happening in my life at the moment.

Devangeo Hicks

Since mama's departure, I felt like I was trying to please my uncle by continuing my education in school because he was helping me financially because it was something that he said she would want and I didn't have much at that time, so I went along with it. I forced myself to do whatever it is to cover this feeling and pretend that everything was amazing. Between dealing with my own personal issues and constantly getting into big arguments with my family that would blow up out of proportion whether it was with my brothers, cousins, aunts or uncle and their opinion of me after all these years.

One of my cousins was so rich and up on her high horse she looked down on others as if they were beneath her or something. She would pass any kind of criticism she could and take jabs at me simply because of whatever reason. At that point in my life, I felt like, if you see me doing bad or either going down the wrong path, why not extend me a helping hand instead of making it seem like you're trying to throw shade or criticize me? Which was exactly why I slowly started to distance myself from some of them, and now I'm slowly distancing myself from a few more as well.

It's sad when you either live for someone else instead of living for yourself or just have toxic people around you that seem like they try to drain and suck all the life out of you like leeches. I'm to the point now where I don't need any of that in my life, and I'll remove it within a heartbeat.

Over these past few years, I have learned to do more myself than I have in my whole lifetime and to be more independent by getting things done on time, the way that they should be because I'll never get anywhere depending on someone else because I'm on their time

I'd often ask my cousin, who I go to school with and who I know always had my back and best interest at heart, about something if I don't have a complete understanding of it. We have never passed any judgment or threw any shade at one other because that's not what either of us is about except for that one time when somebody tried to come between us with some, he-said-she-said stuff. We almost fed into it, but then we realized that this person was only trying to pin against each other because they knew we had a close relationship than what I had with them, so we completely ignored it.

All of the things that I have been through over the years molded me into the fierce young man that I am today. Now I'm not perfect by any means nor do I try to because I still have things to work out within myself, but I'll eventually get to where I need to be with God by my side.

I've grown more and more each day and matured quite a bit since all of that took place, even though I was already mature for my age and wise above my years before then. As the year 2015 came to a close, things started to get much better for me, although that one year mark was upon us that current year since mama's passing; things weren't as bad as I thought it would've been as that day came and went, so after that I started to feel a sense of relief like a heavy weight that I was carrying had been lifted off my shoulders now that I had finally started to accept the fact that she gone and wasn't coming back and to move forward with my life and live it to the fullest. It's like I started become more naïve to the fact that she wasn't here with me and that miserable pain that I felt that whole year started to set side after a while, and I could get back to being me. I knew she never left me and that she was always with me in spirits, I just still wanted the physical part of her here with me.

12

No More Grieving

As the year 2016 began to roll in, in full effect, I started to look more toward the positive side of things instead of putting my energy into the negative. My cousin and I had our ups and downs in classes yet again, but we stayed at a steady pace to try and keep up that time around, but still, it winded up to be another difficult semester. We had this one foreign teacher we took for a national government class, but we winded up failing him because we stopped showing up to his class right along with a math class that we were having trouble in as well.

Our math class was compressed from front to back and it was hard for us to learn anything because it is overpopulated. Everyone mostly stayed on their phones throughout the entire class period, not paying attention to anything else going on around them. Then you had the students who sat in the front every day and who would make an attempt to learn. We never made it to class on time to get front seats, but we weren't trying to sit in the front anyway because the teacher could look right directly at us if we pulled out our phones while they were trying to teach.

The school year proceeded through and my grades looked completely horrible at this time. I remember having two F's because we never dropped out classes before we stopped showing up, but we couldn't anyway because we had to have a certain number of hours, so that it wouldn't affect our financial aid. I began summer school over the summer right along with trying to balance my new job I had just landed working at Rite-Aid. My first set of classes were online, so it was kind of easy for me to try and juggle my way through classes. I worked day in and day out in order to submit the assignments that just seemed unnecessary at the time, and some of them I didn't understand, so I had to use Google to at least get somewhat of an understanding as to what I was supposed to do. It literally wore me out, trying to figure out what some of the assignments were even talking about in the first place, so I had to really critical think my way through and put some stuff together, hoping that it fit well with each other. That's just how hard college life was for me, and not only me but for a lot of people who struggle their way through like me.

I had to take another course online since I have failed the 3rd and 4th semesters because of a careless mistake I made during the final exam. That was before my mama passed away. I had the same teacher except that, this time, he was online instead of teaching inside a classroom, which was good because that man could talk on and on about stuff that would bore people half to death and put them to sleep. Since I had taken the exam before, I already knew what to answer this time but I'm still cautious because it's going to be an online exam this time. After submitting all my assignments at the end, I waited anxiously for the grades to be posted because I always tend to second guess my work and not just in school but overall. I came out of both classes with Cs although I was shooting for higher in one of them. If it's one thing I've learned is that every time I try to shoot even higher for something, I always get the same results with me getting a C, which was okay with me because it meant that I didn't have to take them all over again.

I only had one class for the second session that was held inside a classroom. It was only one, and it was late in the evening, so I could easily go to work and head to class at five o'clock. I then ran into an error where I could only open because, by the time I would get out of my class, I wouldn't have any hours with the class ending at 7:50 and the store closed at 10, which was right up my alley because I hated closing anyway.

At first, it seemed as if the managers were trying to make me decide between my schooling and my job. My first option was school even though I was already over my classes at the time. I didn't want to quit my job because it was my only way of living to sustain myself; plus, I had gotten the job a couple months at the end of the spring semester before even attending summer school. I didn't worry or stress about it because I knew what was meant for me, was for me.

After not worrying about the situation or even having a care in the world, God worked everything out in my favor and turned all of it around for me in the end, so that I could continue making my own money. I got to keep my job, and they made it fit around my school schedule, especially since I only had that one class that second session, which was way over in the day.

The math teacher we took during the summer session was pretty cool and had this laid back vibe, but you could tell he didn't play and we found that out a lot sooner than later. The only downside to that was that he just talked too damn much about the students at the school and how sorry they could be a lot of the times when it comes to going to class and actually doing what their supposed to do. He called them a bunch of sorry-ass Negros that don't want nothing out of life but walk the streets and smoke weed with their britches hanging low and females walking around with their shorts up to their behind, trying to get the sorry-ass Negros's attention.

We felt like he was talking about a lot of us in there, but we were like we actually going to class; now we may slack off, but we go. He said that the other math teachers in the department said that a lot of us were flat-out dumb and don't know how to do shit, and can't even answer a simple math problem, and that it was just pitiful for some of our overgrown asses who were supposed to be college level and can't even solve something so simple as that. He also stated that one teacher suggested that he give his entire class an eighth grade level math test and watch the majority if not the whole class fail it. He went on and on for about an hour, letting us know what was said behind our backs by all of those teachers in the math department. He even said he get a lot of backlash for that, and that they told him that he needed to get strict on us because a lot of teachers say that the only reason everyone tries to get into his class was because they knew he's the most lenient one of all of them, which was true, but he didn't bite his tongue letting us know that.

You could actually tell that he cared about a lot of us because, if he didn't, he wouldn't have shown up that late in the day just to teach us. After preaching for about an hour, he then leveled with us and said that if we meet him halfway, then he'll meet us the rest of the way. We had to actually put forth effort and show that we were committed to his class with it being so late in the evening and not take an advantage of him. I think that after talking with the other teachers and hearing how they would talk to him, he started to feel like the students were actually using him to a certain extent, but that was never my intentions. Everyone knew what we they needed to do, so that we could pass his class because had we not, he would've canceled the whole class and we would've been stuck taking one of the others that talked about us so badly. Other teachers that showed up really didn't care if we got it or not, as long as they were collecting a check from us, they could care less about what we had going on. He also spoke facts about a lot of students that don't do anything but make the university look bad because, if you were to walk around campus, you'd see some of the guys sitting around outside the dorm room buildings, rolling up a blunt, passing it to one another and smoking. Some would come to class with the strong scent of weed in their clothes that had everyone looking around, which was just plain disrespectful to not only us students who didn't smoke, but the teachers as especially.

I remember coming out my room a lot of days when I stayed on campus my first two years and all you could smell was weed up and down the halls. I inhaled so much of the smoke back then. I'm surprised I didn't catch a sickness as I pass through a lot of people who were smoking. It kind of made us students at the university look like we weren't learning anything, and people just roam the campus doing whatever; plus, it was already an open campus, so anybody who didn't go to school with us could just walk into campus and fit in like a regular student. You really can't tell who went to school with us, because the campus is open to anyone who entered. Sometimes it caused a lot of the gunning even visitors that entered the campus still no luck.

As the summer session came to an end, I ended up with yet again, another C average, which I guess I can say was still pretty good. He knew how to teach some math, and he actually engaged with everyone in the class and made us interested in learning something math-related because, let's be honest, a lot of people suck at math if it didn't have anything to do with money, and I was one of them. Oftentimes, I start to think that the students weren't always the problem when it came to learning something of some sort in the classroom because a lot of the teachers would show up and just talk for an hour and twenty minutes just to pass the time because they knew, regardless as to whether we learned anything or not, that they were going to still get paid at the end of the day. So sometimes, I wouldn't just point the finger one way when some of them aren't necessarily doing their jobs as professors either.

He actually made us want to learn something because of the way he taught us while making it easier for us to understand and get the full meaning behind what he was teaching us.

To this day, I still remember everything he taught us during that summer session, which is unlikely for someone like me because I normally forget a lot of material taught, especially those dealing with numbers, after about a few months of learning it. But it's something that I'm working toward getting the better at because that may very well be my downfall later on in life.

13

Second-guessing College

As summer school came to a close, we had a few weeks left to rest before the school year picked back up, and I could barely function properly.

I didn't want to go back to doing all that homework and going back to the same ole, same ole all year around and the thought of even starting again in another couple weeks after we had just gotten out made my mind wonder even more at the fact that we were going to have to read them long chapters, especially since we had just started to get into our major courses.

I felt like I was going to school just to be going, and that's not a feeling anyone should have, especially when you're doing the best you can to make a better life for yourself. It seemed as if I was faced with more obstacles as the school year started off.

I began the fall semester with this chip on my shoulders from not knowing what my future held for me. I came into that semester with this feeling of doubt and fear of not knowing if I was gone even be able to make it. It's like my brain had completely began to shut down and stopped functioning on me when it came to anything school related, I stopped applying myself like I should've because my mind-set just wasn't where it needed to be at that time.

I would always show up and leave early with the mind frame developing if I should even stay in school or just drop out and go from there. My grades hadn't been the best in quite some time then, but as I stopped going, my grades slowly became F's in just about each course. My cousin and I were both faced with this difficult yet challenging situation in our lives because she was just trying to work, and school started getting in her way as well. You could tell we were really close, because, if something affected one, it affected the other one. Both of us was at the point where we were feeling like school was draining us, and we got sick of all the bullshit reading material that we didn't understand or couldn't quite comprehend and it is kind of hard to grasp since there is a lot of the materials that were being taught and reading two or three chapters was just useless for me. You could pretty much say that she and I were like Velcro because, if you see one, nine times out of ten, you were going see the other. That's just how we were because we had that tight bond as kids growing up, which is what you sometimes need just to know that you're not alone because I felt like I was for so long after losing Mama.

I had this part-time job, working as a cashier at Rite Aid, trying to stack some money and save up some, so I could possibly quit school and leave without letting anyone know but my uncle because all of the pressure I was putting on myself started to be too much for me. I was clocking a good bit of money while trying to be a full-time student, but it still wasn't enough for me. Although the job I had kept some money in my pocket, it still was chump change, but I didn't have any bills, so I could manage it a bit better than what the average person could, so I didn't complain on that part because I still had money in my account. I just wasn't happy about the situation I was put in because with that came consequences with me cooking for everybody in the house like they had a disability or some. It's like they just sat back and did whatever, whether they sat on the phone talking to their women while I'm over the stove cooking a meal or some. I did all of that to keep my uncle happy in a way because I felt like, he do anything for me, so I'll return the favor by showing my appreciation toward him by cooking, until it seemed like it was becoming an everyday thing with him just sitting in the chair, kicking back, doing absolutely nothing.

Later that year, around the time of registration for the spring classes, my grades were nothing but basically Fs to the point where I had to drop the majority of my classes for that semester while registering for new ones. Two of my professors both told me that I needed to drop my classes in that semester I was already enrolled in immediately once

Life's Scars and Wisdom

I register for my next set of classes because it was the last day to drop them and they didn't want those grades to appear on my transcript. They recommended I drop, so those Fs wouldn't appear on my transcript and mess my GPA up and affecting my financial aid for the spring semester because it was too late to make up any of the work that I had missed from the other months and to just try again that upcoming semester. I only kept the class I knew the teacher would give me a D in because he was lenient to all of his students, and I knew he wouldn't actually fail anybody to begin with that could intentionally mess them up in the long run considering the situation I was already in.

We weren't halfway through the semester before I stopped going to all of my classes I was taking a little after school first started. I stuck with that one class, so I wouldn't have to repeat the registration process all over again because it would've made it seemed like withdrawing from the university as a whole, and that would've been something else on my plate to worry about. I was so mentally that I didn't want to do anything if it had to deal with school back then. I would easily make up excuses to my uncle during that semester as to why I wasn't attending class for that day. I would always say things like, "We're not going having class because our professor didn't show up or some" although, sometimes, they really didn't show up, but the majority of the time. I was lying to keep him satisfied that he thought I was involved and protected in school, even when he would sometimes piss me off. Around this time, his grandkids came to the house more often than usual.

One thing turned into another with them constantly starting to come every day they get a chance. I honestly thought they started coming around because they saw that he had money and he would do anything for them. It's like he took on the role of playing a parent when he didn't have to. The man would literally give anybody his last, and I'm not going to lie. I couldn't stand it because I knew the intentions that they had, but he didn't even much care about any of that. It's like he was being gullible and just wanted them around more, even if that meant they were eating his pockets. I felt as if those kids were only coming around for the moment to see what they could possibly get from him, and it drove me insane to the point that I wish I could've just erased myself from this man's life without having anything else to do with him whatsoever. Then I had to ask myself, Is it worth me walking around here, being unhappy, carrying the weight on my shoulders because things are changing since Mama's departure? Mad at the world because of something I couldn't seem to change or had no control over, even if he knew the truth and tend to just ignore it. To me, he took care of the kids more than the actual parents did because, every time they needed something, the first thing they would do was "Call Pawpaw," as they say. They didn't come around when mama was in the picture, so I thought it should've stayed that way or that it should've at least been some sort of boundaries established from the start.

Dealing with all of that and school not going so well for me, I didn't know which way to turn or who to turn to in that feeling of depression. Some would've thought that I was jealous of some kids, but I had no reason to be jealous of the in any capacity of my life. I was just opinionated about that and voiced how I felt because right is right and wrong is wrong. I was in no position to move out, so it was pretty much like I was at a standstill in my life, and for the longest time, I would always tell myself that I was going to end up being stagnant to the point where I'm going to always need him. It seemed as if things didn't get better for me in any shape or form and I hated it! I just needed somebody to vent to that would understand where I was coming from in that matter. I didn't really have that, so I had to cope through other ways by just shutting people out because I thought no one really cared. They just made their slick ass comments and went about their day like they normally do. The end of the semester was there and grades were due. I didn't really have to check my banner web account because I already knew what I had in those class. I had that hunch that I had a D in the class that I didn't drop, but I checked my account just to make sure. I knew he wouldn't just flat out fail me because he was so easy going and didn't really have the intentions of failing his students which I think that's why we all tolerated him with his shady ass remarks he made towards the majority of us. I knew he wouldn't just give me an F to completely mess up my GPA or financial aid like that although I deserved it because of the slacking and absences that I did. My grades weren't always the best when it came to my average, but I always managed to stay in good standing throughout my college history.

As I logged into my Banner Web account that day to look at my grade for his class, knowing that he gave me a D, but I just needed that one piece of confirmation that he did, so I could move from forward from there. I actually think that's what kept me off academic probation, which I'm glad it did because I couldn't afford to pay out of pocket for the expense that came with it, but my uncle could. I was just the type of person that didn't want to put my burden and all of my problems on someone else for my foolish mistakes and actions that I did to myself when all of it could've been avoided. With me working as a cashier and being as young as I was, it didn't really bother me as much that I didn't perform well because I knew what I did and didn't do.

A part of me started feeling guilty because I had stopped caring about school as much as I did around that time because it was so hard for me to really get back into the swing of things and stay focused with my mind being all over the place, thinking that I was never going to graduate or even come close to finishing like I should. I was always thinking the worst of every situation that hit me because it seemed like nothing positive was happening in my life, and everything started to seem like it was taking a fall. Then a thought occurred to me, "Do I really want to finish school or just call it quits?"

One thing I've noticed is that people can put a lot of pressure on you when they see you trying to better yourself, and sometimes, it just begins to be too much on a person's plate because some always want to throw their two cents in when it was not needed or asked for. A lot of people always felt that, since my grandma raised me out of all her children and grandchildren, they felt the need to validate or give comments on what I should do or how I should, which explains the relationship that I have with them today.

I was already at a standstill, and then watching my uncle being taken advantage of by his so-called grandbabies made me feel like I was on the verge of a horrific meltdown. For a while, I felt anger and rage because these people were never really in his life and he never really had anything to do with them, until their daddy (my uncle's son) started bringing them over, so now I'm looking around like why all of that had to change all of a sudden. They just knew he had money and saw him as a money magnet, so they made their move and their so-called daddy didn't make it any better with his childish ass antics being that he almost 40 years old.

    I felt like they were just a bunch of con artists doing whatever their dad was telling them to do. On top of that, there were people who would pop up at the house all the time we had never seen before when mama was here, that's why I say she not only played a significant impact in my life, but his as well. That by itself gave me the determination I needed to stay in school and put forth more effort when it came to my going to class every day like I should and actually try to learn something, even if it seemed like things weren't working in my favor. I told myself to give it one last shot and go through with it, and if didn't work out, I would then save up enough money for me to find an apartment, move, and step out on faith with the amount of money that I had already saved up in my account. I can honestly say that, after having a good talk with God about my performance and everything else that I had been feeling lately, it seemed like it was completely falling apart, and he then showed me that things would soon turn around for the better.

14

Picking Back Up Where I Left Off

After being out of school for the holidays and having some time to think to myself and clear my head. I then decided to return that following semester to finish what I started because I knew somewhere deep down that if I didn't finish, something wouldn't sit right with me if I didn't return because I had already owed the school a lot of money for previous semesters, so it would've been a complete waste of time all these years I had gone.

I quit my job at the beginning of the year and walked out about week before school started back because I got into it with one of the store managers about her smart- mouth and slick comments she always made. I thought everything was cool, although I was never really feeling her and her vibe that she had with her nose always being turned up like somebody owe her something. When she got in my face talking to me as if I was a child is where she messed up at. She got all in my face, which was already disrespectful to begin with. I tried to let it slide, but after so many attempts, I'm only going to let a person go so far before they pressed the wrong button in me.

I let her know where to get on and where to get off at real quick because I'm not the type of person you can just go there with without me saying anything back. I could tell I pissed her off after saying what I had to say and just by me laughing in her face, but I didn't give a damn about that job anymore or anyone of the coworkers working there. I had been putting up with their shit ever since I had first started, which I'm surprised I kept quiet for so long. I've always been quick to defend myself because no one else have been there to do it for me, so when she finally pressed the wrong button, I was ready to self-destruct. My thing is I don't bother anybody, and when somebody comes for me and I didn't send for them, they won't like my response in return. Deep down, I felt like it was a set up to begin with, because, after we had shared our words, she then said she was going to call the head manager on me as she proceeded toward the office to call her the manager over us. I thought it was strange how the head manager couldn't answer my text or phone call before the argument had even got to that point, but responds to my text right after I walked out and said that I quit. She probably texted the manager just to see how far I would go, and they wanted to see how everything was going to play out in the end.

I think they were actually glad that I quit, or at least she was because she had gotten me written up several months before that because of another altercation that happened with her. I could sometimes be sloppy on the job, or I just didn't care to be there half the time, but I did make the best of that experience, from what I've learned working being in retail. So, then I was jobless, which didn't matter because I was getting ready to put my focus back into school anyway and I was starting to lose myself and who I was, working at that place just for a minimum wage paygrade.

I think it's important to never lose sight of who you are as a person because then you'll just be stuck, and that's exactly how I was starting to feel. A couple days after New Year's, classes picked back up right after. A part of me didn't want to repeatedly go through the whole class process anymore, but I had to tell myself to just do it and try to be more persistent when doing it this time. I didn't go that first day back, so I missed class that day and waited to go two days later since I only had classes on Tuesdays and Thursdays. I wasn't doing anything important; I just didn't want to go the first day back. When I first walked into class with my cousin that rainy Thursday morning, the classroom was empty, and the professor wasn't in there, but I kind of had that feeling that he was going to say something smart as soon as he walked through the door because that's just the type of person he was and it would kind of come off as him trying to be a sarcastic asshole to us just because he knew he could. As he walked in the class, the first person he looked at with a smirk on his face was me, and his remark to me as soon as he walked into the class good enough was, "Hicks, I didn't think you were coming back. Stand up and state your name and why you chose social work as your major." The class started giggling soon as he asked me to state why I was a social work major as I sat there with this blank look on my face, like I know damn well he not talking to me. I started not to get up because I already knew what was coming next, and then it occurred to me that he was just trying to get a reaction out of me in the first place, just to see how far he can go. I'm not gone lie; he and the class almost got that unexpected reaction that they were looking for. I just knew I was in for an earful about what he had to say about my grades and why I stopped coming to class the semester before that, which was none of his business in the first place, but I continued to hold my tongue and peace.

He gave me a hard time the first couple of weeks back in the semester with his slick comments and remarks, but eventually, he lightened up on me after he saw my effort and determination to continue coming to class, and that was all because of the choice I made the semester beforehand. He would always say things on the sly, like, "Some of you all only coming for a refund and we won't hear from you anymore afterwards."

It took every breath deep in my body not to say anything back to him or to feed into anything he was saying because my mouth can be a like a lethal weapon and my words could cut just as sharp as the next person's. I knew what I had to say would've been very out of line and disrespectful and I wasn't raised to disrespect my elders, but he had it coming, especially since I was trying do right by him and keep my cool, right along with a bunch of other things I had on my plate. It's like he came to class just to get a rouse out of people and pick on them just because he knew he could get away with it or some sort.

He didn't say a word to my cousin, probably because she didn't take him that current semester for any classes, or he just simply thought, "I better not say anything to her because she might curse me out for real so I'm going to pick on the next one."

The fact that we had to take him at eleven in the morning for a statistics class and then again later that day for a policy class. We had at four o'clock that evening. It's like I couldn't win for losing in that situation, so I just went with the flow of things and how the cards were dealt to me.

Only God knew if I was going stay in school that time around or not because it went through my mind to stop coming again and to be done with it because I just felt like I was putting my time and energy into something that seemed like it was never going to happen in the first place. Then with him picking on me didn't make the situation any better.

The teachers in the department started getting onto us about how we acted in public because, they said, that would give them and our school a bad name, and they didn't want that on them, in which I can't blame them for that. They'd often get together in the conference room and talk about some, if not all, of us as opposed to who they think was going to make it and who they think might not just from overall academic performance on tests. And I thought that I was going to be one of them, based on the low percentages I would often get when it came time to take a test. This was exactly why I had stopped going to class in the first place. I felt like I didn't know enough to keep going and that I was wasting my time even trying when I could've been doing something else with my spare time.

Sometimes you just know when teachers get together and discuss their students, who they think gone make it in the field or not. They used to talk about some of the clothes we'd wear, like the females wearing tight leggings or a shirt that they thought was showing way too much cleavage and they would say, "That's not professional" or "Save that outfit for the weekend." One teacher only got onto me about wearing shirts with the word "Hustle" on it, and that's the same one that would always give me a hard time for no apparent reason. The man would give me a hard time for nothing and would disrespect me at any given time of the day. A voice in my head would always tell me, "He don't respect you, so just curse his ass out and leave." You don't have to stand for any of that, but with me being the person that I was, I continued to stay and toughen it out the way that I should have and I didn't want to have that going through my head that I started school but didn't have nothing to show for it when it all boiled down to it. Where I'm from, people will whisper your success but voice your failures out loud to anyone they come in contact with.

I was able to push through that semester anyway because then I felt as if I would've been quitting again, so I gave myself that motivational talk that I needed to hear every once in a while, even though I had so much on my mind a lot of the times, even when it seem like it was tough to try and get through. Some days were better than the next, but I felt like I couldn't live my life the way that I wanted, for trying to please people all of the time. I was nowhere near finished, and where I'm from, people make a big fuss as to whether or not you're in school and if you aren't, that would always be their go-to when giving someone advice, especially the elderly people and I must say, it kind of rubbed me the wrong way because school is not for everybody, and it almost seemed like they'd belittle you if you weren't trying to get an education, not thinking that some people didn't go because they didn't want to be drowned in all that student loan debt.

The end of the semester came, which was like a relief and a big surprise that I even made it through, especially with all the hell I put up with. As I logged into my account to check my grades, I wasn't as nervous as I was those other semesters before because I knew what I had done and that the outcome was better that time around. I waited till the end of the semester to stop going to my interview class, which was already my second time around retaking the class since the semester before that one.

My grades still weren't good at the end of that semester either, but my perseverance was better that time around when it came to actually showing up and being more dedicated. I was still able to avoid being put on SAP, which was a good thing because I didn't have any money to pay out of pocket.

As summer came, I searched continuously for another job, but I wasn't having any luck at the time. I searched jobs on Indeed and other websites the whole time and couldn't find anything. Other jobs that popped up in the description were kind of confusing because I still didn't understand the description about the job and what all that they do, so I avoided applying for any of those. I then heard Walmart was hiring, but I didn't apply because the last several times

Devangeo Hicks

I applied before that, they would always tell me they weren't hiring when employees that worked there told me otherwise. I even applied for Lowe's, since I was out for the summer with nothing to do and I just needed some extra money in my pockets. I didn't know what my next option would be and I didn't want to do fast food anymore, considering the last experience I had. I didn't know what else to do at that point, so I left it alone for a little while until something else came up. I stalked the website just about every day, looking for new postings, but still didn't have any luck.

A couple weeks after school was back in session, I then got an interview with Lowe's, which came as a shock because the manager was hard to keep up with by him being in and out the place all of the time. The guy then asked me my availability, so I could come in for an interview and we could meet up and talk about why I applied for this position in the first place and then maybe we could move forward from there.

The next day after my nine o'clock class, I had to meet with him about the job and my previous job experiences over the years which I knew wasn't the best. I may have over exaggerated and bent the truth just bit when applying, but they say to fake it till you make it. It's not like I was just completely lying for no reason because most of the stuff that happened to me on the other jobs were what really happened. The manager seemed pretty cool and the atmosphere of the place was kind of laid back compared to a bunch of other work places that I've seen or been at. Everyone seemed to have that positive energy that I needed to be around, considering everything I was battling within myself.

The interview went well, or at least that's what I had thought when leaving the place because we had a good conversation going through the process. He told me that I should be receiving a call soon, and they'll keep me on call if they so happen to have a position open because people were always applying. The look on my face was like, "I thought y'all already had some open spots," which was why I even had an interview in the first place. After a couple days went by and I didn't receive a follow-up phone call or anything or hear anything back from them. I took another route and called for myself, but all I got was the same thing, which was, "He's out right now. Can you call back at a later time?" or "He's not in today or at that moment. Would you like to leave a name and number?" But I knew they never informed him that I called, which began to kind of aggravate me just a little because I needed a job and it seemed like they didn't even care. My gas was limited and I didn't have any money to be doing any pop ups to see if the guy was actually at the store or not, so I just waited on the days I had classes to see if he was actually in. I called and called and got the same results.

Soon I just started to give up, trying to get another job because it seemed like nothing was going right, but I didn't really care. I knew I had help without having to worry too much about nothing, so I was thankful, I just wanted my own money because it was some things, I needed to do for myself. My main goal for that semester was to strive for what I believed in and go for what I know, so I could succeed and bring my grades up because I got tired of repeating that same ole loop like I wasn't getting anywhere. It was my second time taking one class and my third taking another. I told myself that I needed to buckle down if I ever wanted to get out of there and get my life back.

My cousin and I were both at the point where we would do anything to help one another succeed, and we did just what we said we were going to do. We took this sweet older lady who has been in the department for years, but we never came across her until that semester we got ready to take her class. We didn't know what to expect from her because we never know she was in that department and I don't see how we never stumbled across her until that point. I thought she was gone target me out the whole class because I was the only guy taking her class at the moment because the other one, I guess dropped her class and stopped coming. It took some adjusting because it was new and different for the both of us.

She was very nice, and you could tell that she cared about her students although she would tell us all the time that she would fail us in a heartbeat, so we knew we had to be serious when dealing with her. We showed up to her class the majority of the time although she talked throughout the class period, but she made some topics we discussed interesting. On days we didn't show, she would want a valid excuse as to why we weren't in her class that particular day. To me, that actually showed that she cared, but also made me think she was trying to be a little nosey as well, which was fine in my book. We took a test in her class like just about every week, so we stayed having to read that book if we wanted to know what was on the test. I actually read the book when it came to her class but my test grades showed otherwise because I still was failing the tests, so the class as a whole had to strategize on how we would do better on her tests. We would all say that we were going to put together a study group so that we could do better when it came time to take the next one, but no one would put together a group text or even put forth the effort to meet up to study, so we would constantly see the same results every time. We then asked about extra work to see if she would be willing to work with us so that we could possibly bring our grade up by the time the semester ended. She agreed to give us the questions out of the book to answer from which ever chapter we were on at the time. Half the class was doing them and half wasn't, which made it kind of difficult for her to want to work with us in order to bring our grade up because we knew she was willing to help us as long as we helped ourselves.

    Right before finals, everyone wanted to get together to complete the questions that she gave us. Luckily, she was lenient to the point where she agreed to take them even when she didn't want to after trying to get everybody to come together to do them. In our interview and communication skills class, we knew what to expect from the instructor because we had already taken the class two semesters before then and failed both times. The only reason we had to repeat the course in the first place was because we stopped going to class, and we didn't do the interview video on which we were graded on to see where we were at when it came to dealing with actual clients.

    My cousin and I got together with a friend of ours in a classroom to shoot the videos for our final exam in another class. We had shot several video recordings with our phones to make sure we talked about all the important information that was to his liking and that the information was accurate enough for the client to understand. I was glad to get that out of the way because it seemed as if everything was all due at one time.

Life's Scars and Wisdom

The week of finals came, and my uncle's car had messed up a couple days before for my final exam. I normally would ride with my cousin, but she didn't have a way herself that day, so I asked another one of my cousins, who so happened to be going that way herself, to take the finals, so I caught a ride with her. I just so happen to make it in on time before the professor showed up.

Everyone was preparing our professor's test because we didn't know what was going to be on it. All we know is that it was a fifty-question test because she let us know ahead time. The next week after, I waited to see what my grades were going to be, but I knew that I had a good semester that time around, but it had been a minute since my grades looked decent enough. I had this one class on Canvas, so I could monitor my grade as the professor put his grades in for the interview class that we took. Every time he entered a grade, my phone would alert me as to whether my grade went up or down. All my other grades were posted except his which left me kind of nervous because I didn't know what my grade was going to be with it going up and down the way that it was. I just knew I was going to get a B that time around, but my outcome wasn't what I expected it to be. I ended up with a C in his class as well, but I ended the semester on honor roll, that left me shook because it had been a minute since I even made anything to begin with.

When that spring semester of 2018 hit, I had to keep at a steady pace to try and maintain my GPA since I have done so well that previous semester although, half the time, I didn't attend my eight o'clock class or I came in late because of me not wanting to get up that early. We had the same instructor from our interview class in the fall for our second half of human behavior. My test grades in the class were about average because we had to read about two chapters in there as well, then we would take the tests weekly or, sometimes, every two weeks, because of his lack of showing up to class right along with ours, but I think he had to be worse than us on some days, especially in the beginning. We really didn't just, what you'd say, take him too seriously because he would normally be out of class just about as much as we were. He would constantly put in those group texts he sent us when the semester first started that class was canceled, which was fine by me because I had other stuff to do anyway besides sit in a classroom and listen to him talk for the majority of that period. I remember him telling us a week in advance before the storm hazard came through to read two chapters in our book from where we left off in both classes in our first human behavior class, since both parts required the same book.

Cut to it, we were basically out a whole week, and I still haven't even cracked open the book to even read it or get the slightest understanding of it. I was too busy trying to read and prepare for another class with the same teacher I took several semesters back because the word was going around on how much she had change, since the last time my cousin and I had taken her elective class. I knew that time we had to be on it because we took her for one of the main courses that we needed on the curriculum. Come to find out that next week later, I scored even worse on her test than I did on his, and she was the one I studied and tried to prepare myself for the most. When I came to her to ask about my grade and if there was anything else I could do to bring it up, she told me I have to read. I implied that I did read the book; all of the information doesn't just stick like it should, especially while reading two chapters for her class and another one as well. By the time I even took the test, my mind went completely blank on most of the information I tried to retain from the book. I still didn't get anywhere from asking her if there was anything I could do in the near future when studying for a test. It was like she didn't give a rat's ass if I passed it or not just by her implying that I simply read. In my head I'm like, "That's why I even came to you in the first place to get an insight on how I can better prepare myself when it came time to take another one."

I left the class a little disappointed in myself because it was like I didn't know how to really just sit down and study the material that was given without me forgetting half of what I read. I figured I wouldn't be able to reason with her about my test grade or how I could better prepare myself in the near future.

Life's Scars and Wisdom

As I went to my car and got in, I just sat there for a minute, thinking about my life and what it had eventually came to. I thought my mama, and the thought that I could really be doing something else with my time instead of wasting it on unreasonable teachers that didn't want to work or cooperate with us as students just because of the so-called saying, "We got ours. Y'all trying to get yours."

Although I bit my tongue many semesters on what I had to say, I felt like we as students sometimes seemed as if we were kissing our professors' asses, especially the ones that seemed to be assholes for no reason at all or at least that's how they sometimes came across as if they were. This is why I can tell you that God truly worked a miracle in both my cousin and my favor because the week of registration came for the fall classes, and we went to go get enrolled that morning after our eight o'clock class with everyone else, so that we could get registration out of the way because, if you registered late, you'd have to get overrides, and we weren't trying to have that problem lingering over our heads.

We sat down with our advisor to see where we both were in classes, and we seemed to be right there with one another. As he advised us, he noticed that we only had three classes left to take before entering a fieldwork placement agency, which was beyond me. We knew we were supposed to come out that next spring after, but as we looked through the courses, we noticed that all three classes that we needed were being taught during the summer sessions as well, and a thought occurred to me that we should take those last three classes in the upcoming summer, so we could do field and graduate in the fall instead of that next spring.

We got our alternate pin for the summer classes and the fall, just in case we changed our minds about summer school, but we proceeded through because we were in it together. We made this pact that we were going to start together and finish together, and nothing and no one was going to get in the way of that. Now all we needed to do was make sure that we were good with the current classes we were taking just so we wouldn't mess anything up that would set us back.

Devangeo Hicks

It's like we could finally see the light at the end of the tunnel that we had been in for years now, and I must say, for me to hear something like that was a burden lifted off my shoulders. That then gave me the motivation I needed to go even harder in the classes I was already taking, even when I didn't think I could. I think that and those weekly questions that were given to us, saved me from having to repeat my Practice I class because they were bonus points that added onto our actual grade.

I didn't start passing any of the tests until like close to the end of the semester, so I had to juggle a bit more than the average person, but I wasn't the only one for that matter. Our human behavior class was another story because it was all over the place, and most of the work that was due throughout the semester was due close to the end, which were assignments, such as ecomaps and genograms, the last two chapters to our test, etc., plus the unexpected presentations we had to do in class on a psychiatric unit. It was a bonus for us that he even put the rest of our work online for us because everyone could help each other out with the assignments because over half of us in the class didn't understand the ecomap and genograms and he could tell by our last quiz grade we took in class that showed otherwise. I remember only drawing out some of the information but was nowhere near close to what he wanted in both the diagrams, so I left it alone. He knew that if he put the rest of the work online, everybody was going to get together to help each other out, which was a good idea in my part because he barely showed up to class, and if the majority of us failed the course, they weren't going to look at us; they were going to look at him to begin with about what was being taught in the course and why most of failed the class.

I knew I was gone pass my art class that time around because it was my third time taking the same thing over again. Although my major would've taken a couple Ds that were in my main courses, my instructor still kept putting art in my schedule to retake, but I could see why because he was only trying to help my GPA. Even though that was my third attempt at taking the class, it was my second attempt with that instructor I took the spring before that, and I only went with him again because he seemed like he was the most lenient and the one that will try to level with you unlike the older guy I took two springs before that.

At the end of the semester, I e-mailed my art teacher just to confirm that my grade was a B for his course, and he said yes, so that was out of the way for me. Now all I had to do was worry about my major classes. I knew I possibly had a B or C for the elective class I took under the same instructor I had for the first part of my human behavior class that fall because she didn't believe in failing anyone if they were doing the best they can. Once I saw my grade from her, I was in the clear waiting on just two other classes of mine. The week for grades to post came and I was nervous as to what I got in both those two last remaining classes.

But no other class could come close to how I was feeling about my Practice I class at that time because it's like I knew I passed the class, but then again, I really wasn't sure about this one because the professor that taught that class had me feeling some type of way, especially after she grilled me in my group when we were acting out presentations in front of the class for role play, which was the biggest part of our grade.

When the finals week came and grades were being posted, I drove to the campus because the suspense was pretty much killing me, and I had to know what my grade was regarding that class, so I could get that weight lifted from my shoulders.

I walked in the building and proceeded my way up the stairs because the elevator was getting worked on at that time by maintenance. As I walked down the hall, I saw that her door was slightly open, so I knocked on her door, and she said, "Come in." I nervously walked in with my heart damn near about to beat out of my chest to see what I finally got in her class, so that I could stop checking the Banner Web every second of the hour.

She was actually in the process of putting grades in when I came through the door and getting ready to submit them. She asked, "How can I help you, Mr. Hicks?" even though she already knew what I came in there for in the first place. I asked her what my grade was for her class, and she said that I had a C, which was fine by me! I just didn't want to take the class again because that was going to set me back from graduating in the fall.

Now that all of that was taken care of and squared away, I was waiting for my last grade, but I just so happened to run into my last professor on my way out of the building to ask him what I had for his class, but he was so into his lady friend that he was walking around, introducing her to the other teachers. His response to me was, "I want to know why you and two others in the class have the same ecomap and genogram," and suddenly, he slams the door in my face without even giving me any reason to explain. He had a smile on his face, which seemed unusual because that was the first time I've seen that man smiling ever since because he always comes to class with a scowling look. Everyone in class noticed it and thought he either had issues or something was wrong with him and he needed help since he dealt with a bunch of psychiatric clients, and it seemed that like it was starting to rub off on him, and he was taking it out on us.

I stalked my last grade for his class the next day on Canvas he always somehow manages, being the last teacher to enter grades. We could all look at our grade for his class as he entered them by the alerts that would come to our phones from the app. Every time I got a notification, my heart skipped a beat because my grade kept jumping from an B to a C. I didn't know what to expect because my grade dropped by a bunch after he entered the biggest grade it was to put in, which kind of scared me into thinking that I had already failed. Now if I would've had to repeat this class, it would've had a major impact on me coming out in the fall since that was the second half of that course, and it was only being offered in spring and not that summer and most definitely that fall. Once I saw that I was finally in the clear for his class, I patiently waited the next two weeks for summer school to start, but it came so quick.

15

Summer School and Field Placement

As I entered the class, I saw a few people who I normally have classes with and some who were ahead of me and were supposed to come out with the spring class that had just graduated but failed that second half of that Practice II class, so they had to wait. We had that same instructor that we had for the first half of the class, which didn't make it any better because we all knew how she was coming.

As she came in the classroom, I saw this big book that she had in her hand. I just knew that was going to be a shit ton of work she was getting ready to have us do for the next six weeks.

She passed out the calendar for that month that had everything planned and mapped out on what we were going to be doing each week and what she expected from us. It seemed like it was a bunch of work at the time, but I can honestly say it truly wasn't when looking back at it now. It was like we were basically squeezing a semester full of work into one month, which made it kind of got overwhelming just by looking at what we had to do.

This time around, we had to do timelines from two different books instead of answering questions from just one, and they were due every Tuesday and Thursday of the week since we had to meet up with our groups on the Mondays and Wednesday's part of the week.

We didn't have a lot of money, considering we didn't have enough aid left from the previous semester to cover us for everything and having to pay the rest out of pocket, so my cousin and I put our heads together and looked online to see if we could find the books for a cheaper price because, college textbooks are extremely expensive for whatever the reason maybe. We found the book on an app for a really cheap price and hopped right to it, considering the fact that we needed the book ASAP.

After purchasing the book, we immediately had work due two days after, so it was a process just getting it done and having it completed so we wouldn't have any points taken off because we needed every little point we could get when it came to her class and how she does things. When putting us into groups of four like how she wanted us, I really didn't know what to expect when working with the other three people. I knew them; we just didn't really talk or click like that, but we put our differences aside to get things done, so she wouldn't say anything and try to deduct points from us just by us not getting along with each other.

The constant meeting up for presentations is what threw me off because I didn't want to do a presentation every single week, but I knew not to complain or say anything out of the way even though I wanted to at times.

We took our tests on the chapters the same day we presented to the class. It was a struggle, trying to get to campus on time enough to print our timelines out and have whatever we were going to say written down, so it looked like we knew exactly what we were talking about while standing in front of the class talking.

I did pretty well on the presentations because I didn't feel pressured to be precise and worry about how I was going to do. The only time I really messed up was when I started explaining something on a slide in front of the class, then I'd go to the next slide and tell some details about the information that I'm presenting on that slide, and I would do this big pause right in the middle of trying to explain it and forget what I was talking about then go onto the next slide without even elaborating a bit more on what I was talking about to begin with. I knew she noticed because she picked up every little thing we did, and she would always seem to have this smirk on her face when she picked up on something and noticed when something didn't seem right. I didn't mind looking at the class while presenting, but I still couldn't get with trying to make eye contact with her even though I did. She didn't seem to grill us that badly during the chapter presentations, but we knew to expect criticism when it came time for the final presentation because it was worth half of our grade for the course, and everybody got graded individually and not as a group.

Two out of the four groups that we were placed in couldn't seem to get along for anything in the world, and you could see it with everyone doing their own part, not caring if the other one got it together. I thought that was going to be me and my group at first, but in the end, we actually got along and came together as a whole to help one another and make sure we were all on one accord.

After acting out the last presentation in front the class, I could honestly say that she didn't have critique on anything, which amazed me because she always had some sort of comment to roll off her tongue.

She passed our grading sheet out, and I saw that I had a B for the class. I couldn't believe what I was seeing right before my very eyes because I thought for sure I was going have to retake it otherwise, but God had seen fit that I didn't.

Once that was over and done with, we had our five o'clock class to worry about because we had yet again another presentation, we had to present in front of the class individually that time, which was called an immersion project. Some of us didn't seem to understand how to do it or even know start it off for that matter because I know I didn't. In that class, we talked about different cultural backgrounds and ethical behavior from different people all over the world and what their beliefs were.

His class was like four days out of the week like every other class, but he changed it to us only having to meet up two days of the week. He then put together a group message for us, so that everyone could all stay connected and know what was going on. When we met up for class, he didn't show up or anything after the first day, so we were looking around, wondering where he was because his car wasn't on campus at the time either. He then put in the group message that we weren't going to be meeting for his class that day, which made us have to come back the next day until he decided to just change the whole course to an online class and all of our work would be online from then on, although he did state that on the last day of class, we would all meet up in person that day to do our final presentations.

I thought we should've just done the project and submitted it on Canvas, but he wanted to see what we know face to face, but I wasn't feeling it because the topic that I was given was difficult. I could hardly find information on the topic when trying to research it to see what it was about. It took me forever to even put my mind on starting on it because I procrastinated on it so much to the point where I literally started on it the night before it was due.

I didn't know if it was right or anything, so I was just taking a chance at doing it, not knowing what the outcome would've been. I was really skeptical about getting up in front of the class to present my assignment to them, just because I felt like theirs would be right and mine would be way off from what he really wanted.

I stayed up till about two in the morning, putting it together, researching information to put in to make it sound right, but I barely found anything pertaining to my topic, so I had to go off what I knew, which was hardly anything.

That next morning, I got up, putting the finishing touches on my slide show to make sure it looked decent enough and that it just wasn't thrown together for nothing. I had a rough draft copy and saved the final copy to my flash drive right after I was done with it. Later that day, I headed to class because I had to print the syllabus receipt to that class since we never got a chance to turn it in because we never had class on campus anymore after the first day, and it was worth five points, and I needed every bit of my points I could get, especially after that presentation because I didn't know how it was gone turn out.

Once I got to class, I saw that he hadn't made it yet, and people were putting the finishing touches to their PowerPoints through their laptops. At first, we didn't know if he was going to show up or not because his car wasn't on campus when I first pulled up, so we were thinking we were going to get a pass and just be able to turn them in on Canvas like the last graduating class did. So as someone mentioned that, he walked right through the door, ready for us to get ready to present. He asked, "So who's going first?"

I thought we were going in order on whatever number we had picked because I was number three. As everyone was getting up to present their immersion projects, I was nervous and eager to get it out of the way because I was tired of the suspense eating me alive as to how I would do on this presentation. As they started to narrow down on the presentations, he started to let people go if they had already done theirs, because it was getting late and everyone was ready to go.

The class only had about four or five people who hadn't gone yet, and of course, my cousin and I were two of the last people that stayed back because we hadn't gone yet. Finally, it was my turn to go, but I felt a little relief because the majority of the class had already left, and it was only him and two other people watching.

As I got up there to present, I had no idea that my presentation was going to crash and burn the way that it did nor did I think that my final copy of my PowerPoint wouldn't save the way that I thought it would have. Before I even left the house, I made sure I clicked save two or three times before taking it out of my computer and heading out the door. The moment I put my flash drive into the laptop at school and I saw my rough copy, I knew then that my presentation would be a fail, and it did. I had my index cards and what I was going to say already written down, but they went with my final copy of the presentation.

I stood up there and presented what I had for about three or four minutes, and at that time, I was like, "Just forget it and give me the F because it was trash." The thoughts that went through my head was like, "I just can't believe this is what happened." I couldn't even use the information that I wrote on the cards because then it would've been a complete waste of my time and his because I didn't have the final copy.

He told me that if I could answer any of the questions pertaining to how my topic discusses at least three issues that was in the syllabus then I was good, but I couldn't think of how my topic related to any of the questions. I instantly got frustrated because I was overthinking the questions, but when you don't know, you just don't know, and I was one of those students that didn't have an answer if I didn't know what I was talking about in particular.

Once he saw the frustration, he then made a deal with me, which was he was going to boost my grade for the project and, hopefully, my grade from the other assignments we did online with the analogies will keep me afloat so that I could pass the class.

After that week, the first session of summer school came to a close, and it was onto the second session. Later, I found out that I passed the class with a B and ended the session on a better note than what I even thought. The last class we had to take before entering our field internship was Integrative Seminar where we had to dress up in professional attire every time we come to class. and some days, she'd let us get away with casual wear, but it was only if she required it. She did tell us that we were not going to be meeting up four days out of the week because she didn't want to be there every single day either, so it seemed as if we were going to have yet another easy class that we could breeze straight through without actually having to worry about a bunch of unnecessary work. We only had to take one test in the whole course for the class, which most of us didn't pass the first time around, so she let us take it again, and we all scored better that second time, so she used the highest grade.

I noticed that once we all got to the end of the curriculum with our classes, the teachers started to be a little more lenient toward us and worked with us more when it came time for us to submit assignments because they knew how hard we wanted to finish school. Plus, we were doing the best we could even if we didn't know what we were doing half the time. She also had us prepare our portfolios outside of class, in our spare time, so that we could present it in front of the class.

Our portfolios consisted of a professional picture on the outside of the binder with our name on it with spring and fall 2018 on it. When you open up the binder, the first thing you would see is our field placement form and over to the right, you'd see our letter to the professor, a resume of the specific jobs that we've worked at over the past few years, the application with our name address, GPA, and our strengths and weaknesses. We had to read our paper out loud to the class on why we chose social work as a major and plans that we are hoping to change and accomplish in the near future as social workers.

I didn't want to do that presentation either because it seemed like it was nothing but presentation after presentation that never stopped throughout summer school. I felt as if I was about to reach my breaking point, trying to cross that finish line that I had been longing for. I wasn't prepared because I had left out a few details in my paper when I was typing it, so I had to make some stuff fit into it just by saying my age and some of my life experiences that had impacted me to make me want to be a social worker. It basically seemed like I was going off the top of my head while combining what I had on my paper into one, so that the class could understand it.

After presentations, class ended about a week earlier than when it was supposed to, but we had to set up an interview with our internships according to where we were placed at. I was lucky to be placed right at home because of an older classmate of mine who graduated the fall before me. I didn't know what I was getting myself into, but I was glad that she was there to help me along the way with my interview process and help me get through. I believe that was God looking out for me all along because he knew I wouldn't have made it being placed at another internship, because I only communicated with a handful of my classmates I graduated with.

16

Fall Internship and Graduation

Glasses were over and done with, but everyone had to do a background check before being fully accepted into field, which I already knew I was going to pass because I didn't smoke or have any criminal background that would've shown up during the screening.

The tests took about a couple days to come back, but once they did, we were in the clear to set our interview up and see how things would go. I called the nursing home to see when it would be a good time to come in since school was like three weeks from starting. My instructor informed me that she would be the one over me, showing me around and what to expect while being at the nursing home. I then called the nursing home to set up a time I could meet with the administrator and talk with her to make sure that it was okay for me to do my internship there. She then called and told me a date that I could come in with my portfolio, so that she could meet me.

I was nervous at first, but seeing that they were very open to having me there with them, I eventually had to break down the barriers I had around me and opened up a bit more since I was going to be interning there for the next three months, and I didn't want to make it seem awkward while being there either.

My instructor signed the few paperwork that I had, and I headed out the door. As time slowly started to wind down and field approaching, I begin to question my ability to be able to do anything right and that soon as I got there, I was going to mess up and be kicked out of my internship and forced to be placed somewhere else, because I didn't understand any of that paperwork that I had to turn in weekly since I never had to do it before.

We went over the paperwork in our seminar class when putting our folders together for field, but nobody fully understood how it was supposed to be done until we actually started. The week before school started that following Wednesday morning, we were told to come in for orientation where a bunch of speakers, and even some students in the master's level program got up to speak about their experiences.

I've never even seen some of the students before, but they had been attending the university for the longest time. I guess because they were so far ahead of me that I hardly saw them anyway because they stayed in class for long hours of the day. I'm not going to lie; after hearing some of them speak and how open they were, it made me feel like I had a lot of work to do when starting field that next week. Some of the speakers were motivational and inspirational even though I was halfway sleep through the whole thing, plus we had to be there by eight that morning all the way until three in the evening. The only good thing was that they fed us breakfast as soon as we got there and lunch, so we didn't have to go anywhere between breaks unless we had something to do.

The fall semester started the next week, and my mind was all over the place, wondering about my life and how far I had actually came despite the odds, and what others said about me, including my own family, that said I wouldn't make it near the end.

As the professor came in, carrying our folders, she welcomed us to the last part of our classes and basically ran down the rules on what they expect while we are in field. She stated that we are to be on time every day like it's an actual job and to dress in a professional manner because she knew how some of us be dressed while walking around campus. She also stated that it's important that we are doing what we are told because they could pop up at any given time to check in on us.

After she went over the syllabus with us, she told us to e-mail her our e-mail addresses so that she could e-mail us a copy with our time sheet on it, our weekly supervision, field placement contract, and etc. My cousin and I went straight to the library to print a few copies of each form, considering that we start field the next day and we wanted to be prepared.

That night before I was anxiously awaiting that morning because I really didn't want to do the whole internship thing, I was not feeling it at all, but I knew I came to far to just quit, especially with graduation being right around the corner. I didn't take any of my sleep-aid pills that I normally take to put me to sleep, so I tossed and turned the whole night through because I knew that if I took the pills, they wouldn't have seen me at eight that morning and that wouldn't have been a good first impression on my part.

That next morning, I woke up with the wrong attitude, sleepy and all, but I knew I had to get it done. I didn't want to go mingle with other people because I wasn't a people person and I didn't get along well with others when it came to any type of communication with anybody in the work field.

My instructor texted me before I even left the house to ask me do I had started field that day, and I replied with a simple "Yes, I'm on my way." I had on a blue jean button-down dress shirt with black pants and a pair of Jordan. I didn't think that through when I was getting dressed that morning, but I really didn't care either. I was just ready to get started so that I could get my degree and put an end to school because I felt like it was ruining my life at one point in time and that I couldn't live my life the way that I wanted to.

I came in, and I can tell my instructor was looking at me kind of funny, but I didn't ask why she was and went about my day just to avoid confrontation. I sat in the office, talking to her for the majority of the day while waiting for her to tell me what I should be doing since I knew my professors was so serious about this field placement that any little fuck up I made could possibly get me kicked out, but a part of that didn't really matter to me because I was doing what I wanted to do in the first place.

I finally stepped out of the office and walked around to get a feel for the place and what it was going to be like since I was gone be interning there for a while, so I had to scope some stuff out and take a look around at there see what role a social worker actually play in nursing home facilities when attending to the needs of the residents.

I was told by the administrator before even starting that I was gone be placed in a certain part of the facility, which was known as the psyche unit. People had mentioned that part of the unit so much and how they can tend to be a bit of a handful, so that was the part I was trying my very best to avoid at all cost, because you never knew what to expect when dealing with those type of people because of their mind state in particular and how they were gone be day to day.

When my instructor first took me back there on the first day, I didn't know what was going to happen as we walked through those doors with this uncertain look on my face. Soon as we walked through those doors, they came out of their room, meddling with everyone that came in there, asking them for cigarettes. I just knew they were getting ready to come toward us since I was a new face they'd never seen before.

Some of them got all in my face, asking me what my name was and a bunch of other questions that got to be annoying and unnecessary. Their breath stunk so bad that I could've thrown up because they didn't believe in brushing their teeth and taking baths every day. One of the guys came up to me, trying to touch all of me, and one of the nurses had to tell him to step back because I was a young man and I didn't swing that way, which I'm glad she did because I didn't know how to react to something as that without being rude about it and saying something I had no business saying, but my facial expressions tell it all, and the nurses could see it all on me while laughing about it. I had to act in a professional manner and tend to what we went in there for in the first place, and that was to pull some information from some of their folders because some things needed to be updated in the social services system.

The psyche unit didn't consist of anything but men the back part of the facility, and they couldn't come out to be with the civilized part of the nursing home because of their behavioral patterns and how some of them would flip out instantly, which I've seen a lot of times I had spent there.

While practicing my social work skills and putting what I had learned in class into play, it still took me a minute to come out of my shell when it came to talking with the staff in the morning meetings and even with some of the residents when they like to walk around cracking jokes with one other. I felt out of place there for a minute until I started getting the hang of things although my instructor was quick to jump down my throat a lot with a bunch of careless mistakes that I made without even thinking about the consequences that both she and I could've gotten in trouble for all because of me.

I got a lecture every single morning about how I needed to do better if I wanted go further in life and stop making excuses for everything. Hearing that quite a bit, I started to get discouraged about even going into that area of work after graduation. Hell, a part of me didn't even think I was going to make it to that day from the way I handled being put in difficult tasks. After a while, it seemed like the mistakes kept repeating itself daily with her asking me to do the most simplest task, and I know she got irritated with me because the average person would've, but I was grateful that she didn't give up on me because she would always say, "Somebody took a chance on me," so she wanted to give me one to show "what I can do."

It got to the point where I didn't want to show up in the morning or I would show up late just because I knew I was going to mess up somewhere along the line. I believe it's because I put so much pressure on myself to try to be perfect that I didn't have the best field experience that I thought I could have even with me being placed at home. I didn't know how to do that weekly supervision paperwork and the journals we had to turn in weekly on Mondays when we had class. She had to sit me down and show me how to do them just for me to catch on and get the hang of how it should be done based on what we do weekly at the facility. I started developing that I-don't-care attitude again about school but suppressed it a little more than usual because I knew how I could be once my mood changed, and I would completely shut down on everybody and act like I'm not there, but with me doing my best to finish what I started. I kept my mouth shut and didn't really speak about it too much because I knew it would just lead to something else.

I stayed in the office with her for the majority of the time I was there and only really came out to fax paperwork or make copies of something. I didn't really give it my all because it's not like I was getting paid and I didn't see the point of doing other people's job when I'm

Life's Scars and Wisdom

not getting anything in return but a grade for it. The thoughts that were going through my head were that I needed to be getting paid something for my time because I was there for eight hours, from that morning to the evening part of the day. By the time I got out, the day was basically over with, so it really got me to wondering, "Do I really want to work a nine-to-five job the rest of my life?"

Our professor did tell us in Integrative Seminar that we will know if this was something that we wanted to continue doing by the time field was over. Then it occurred to me that I had been putting my dreams on hold for something such as this for the longest, and I wasn't always happy about it, but I continued to do what I do, and that was to finish stronger than ever.

That Thursday morning, I didn't have to come in as early as I thought I would, but I did go with two of the staff members to help decorate for the annual Olympics that they had every year. When asked by one of the staff members if I wanted to go help and set everything up, it was against judgment because I'm like, "I didn't come here for all of that," but I went anyway to get out of the office since I had been sitting there doing school paperwork since that morning I got there.

As we pulled up to the coliseum, we had to wait for this guy, who used to work at the nursing home, to come with the decorations for us to start putting everything together. After sitting there for an endless amount of time waiting on him, I was over the whole thing and just wanted to go home because it was after field hours for me.

After the guy finally showed up, we had to bring the decorations in to set up in the spot they had us placed at. They couldn't decide how they wanted to place the decorations, which made it even more annoying and frustrating because we had been down there an hour waiting on the guy to show up. Right after getting everything that we had set up and into place, it was time to go, but little did we know, there was another problem awaiting us outside, and that was a flat tire.

We didn't know where or how it all came about because she didn't hit anything on the way down there that we knew of, so she called her brother-in-law, and we waited for him to come patch the tire up so we could go. I'm thinking we were about go home, but we had to make another stop at Walmart after leaving the coliseum because we had to stop and find the residents some clothes for the next day, so they could look presentable. After being there for almost forty-five minutes, trying to find sizes for the residents in the clothes that they wear, we then proceeded on our way home.

I fell asleep in the back because we had literally been gone just about all day, so I was just ready to go home and get in my bed at that point. We didn't make it back to the nursing home until about nine o'clock that night, and all I could think about was crawling in my bed and going to sleep, seeing as I had to be back up there at seven that morning because we were scheduled to leave at about eight that morning and be at the coliseum by nine. I was told to wear a red shirt to blend in with the rest of the nursing home staff members that attended since that was one the color shirts everyone else was wearing. Of course, we didn't leave on time the morning after for whatever reason by it being a lot of stuff going with some of the residents not wanting to cooperate.

One resident decided he was not going at the last minute, so I got his shirt and put it on over the one I was already wearing. Both the facility buses finally drove around to pick up the residents, so we could head out to our destination. The thought that was going through my head was, "I could've stayed at home a little longer and slept if I knew we were leaving this late."

I rode with the same two staff members I was with the day before and right along with someone who was just like a cousin to me through marriage. I think they wanted me to drive the van I was in at first, but then told me I could ride with them, which was right up my alley because I didn't have the gas to be driving that broken-down van out of town.

When we got there, I saw that the parking lot was packed from the front to back with nothing but people coming in left to right. Lord knows I didn't want to be social with anybody, but I had to put my game face on because I knew I had to be there, so I had to suck it up and just try to get through the day by all means. Being there for a minute, I started looking around for my cousin because I knew we were both going to be at the same location since she was placed in a hospice facility in that area with another classmate of ours.

Next thing I knew, I saw a lady walking around, handing out this stale-ass popcorn, so I decided to grab a bag not knowing it had been out a minute. I went to sit down and look up; here comes my cousin and classmate walking toward me.

We walked around for a bit before the games started, then I had to report back to where I belong before they start looking for me and wondering where I went. The speaker, who hosted the annual Olympics, came out and spoke on how sports doesn't build character and a bunch of other motivational words that just made you pay attention to what he was saying. Some of the staff members went to pick up the pizzas they order ahead of time from Pizza Hut, so they could feed the residents and everyone from our facility who attended.

The event lasted up until two o'clock that afternoon, but we sat there for about forty-five minutes, waiting for the transportation bus to pull up, so they could put the residents back on board and head back safely.

On the way back, we stopped, and I got me some Five Guys, which is like this place that serves homemade burgers and fries that had so much Cajun seasoning on them that just from looks of them, it would give you high blood pressure. They had several boxes of pizza left from the event, and they tried to offer me some, but I didn't want any because I had lost my appetite after I went in the public restrooms at the coliseum. The bathrooms were completely filthy when you first walk in to the point of where I had this look of disgust on my face. All you could see and smell was piss all over the bathroom floor which was one of the most unsanitary things you could do. It turned my stomach so bad, I'm surprised I was even able to eat later that day. Seeing the prices at Five Guys were through the roof made me rethink that pizza situation, but I bought it anyway because I had never had it before and so many people would talk about how good it was, so I tried it.

I spent twelve dollars on a burger and fries I didn't even eat, not including the drink because everything was sold separately. But I was cool about that because they had drinks left over from the event sitting in the cooler, so I grabbed one of them.

We made it back around three that evening, and I stuck around long enough to help them unload the stuff they had from the car because they were going to feed the rest of the residents the pizza that didn't get to attend the Olympics because of their condition. My instructor never came towards that way that day, so I hopped in my van and left.

The first week of field wore me out because it was something that I knew I had to get used to for the next three months of being there, despite how I felt in that moment. I didn't realize how drained I was until I got home later that day to take a short nap, and ended up sleeping the rest of the day away with my alarm repeatedly going off, but I never heard it.

My first week there wasn't as bad as I anticipated it to be, but the constant mistakes started come in the week after. It seemed like **every** time she asked me to do something, I'd find a way to mess it up, because it's like I was always afraid and feared whatever task she gave me. I was lucky that I knew her beforehand and that she was so laidback and understanding because, if it had been someone else, I would've been out the door the first week.

As field started roll on, the presentations about the facility was coming up, and I was nervous about presenting in front of the class because I didn't know how everything was going to turn out. I had to prep through about a week or two in advance just to make sure I covered everything she had on the syllabus. I already knew how she nitpicks through things if something wasn't right and I wanted to be prepared in the best way as possible. I went through the facility's website and scrolled through it, taking the bits of information I've seen and copied and pasted it onto my PowerPoint and changed some words up to fit my description. Some of the information I couldn't seem to find, so I had to backtrack and ask my instructor as to how she got the information she needed when she had interned there that fall before me. She came in very handy with some of the information she used, like printouts from different websites. With that I was able to paste some things together to make it work because I was real big on googling things and making it fit in some kind of way. I used Google a lot of the times being that I was in school, but she knew how to pick out certain words in order to find information about whatever it was that she needed, so she was very helpful to me when I really needed some help. Plus she had already been through it before me, so I was very appreciative of the help that she provided me with. I had put together the majority of the slides, but I still needed certain pieces of information about the facility that would help me through the presentation because I didn't feel like answering a whole bunch of questions that I didn't know the answer to in front of the class. I had to think fast and ask my cousin if I could use her laptop since I didn't have one at the time, so I could finish. I went to personal friend of mines that worked at the facility as an assistant and had her look over my information of what I already put on the PowerPoint so far.

She helped me reword some of my sentences as I made a few errors here and there when typing it out and looking back over it. After sitting there, trying to get my stuff typed out for about an hour, here comes another one of my cousins and her badass kids who didn't have any home training, messing up my train of thought because all they wanted to do was play and snatch on the chords of the laptop. The look on my face I gave her was like, "Get your badass kids before I whoop them" because the laptop I was using to begin with wasn't mine.

After being down there for about three hours total, I left with confidence, knowing that I did my best and that I had covered most of the information, so that was a plus for me. I knew how hard I worked on it, so she couldn't say I didn't put forth the effort. I then sent it to my cousin, who I was going to school with and had her look over it for, just to make sure it looked okay and I didn't need to go back to add anything else extra.

When she finished looking over my PowerPoint, she put some decoration to it because it was plain, and just by her doing that, it brought out my presentation even more and made it look better, like I actually put some thought into it, even though I did. The morning before class, I looked over all my work just to make sure everything went together and was set in motion before heading to school to print everything out. I had to pick out the dressy clothes that I was going wear to make sure I looked presentable or at least decent because I knew she would say something about what we had on and whether it looked presentable or not.

I put my clothes on and headed out the door toward campus about an hour and a half earlier because I knew how it was going to be with

Devangeo Hicks

not only just me but my classmates and other people all over campus trying to print at one time for the classes as well.

Once I got to campus, I seen a whole swarm of people headed to the computer lab printing out information on what they needed for their classes as well. There was hardly anywhere to sit, so I stood for a minute, waiting for someone else to get up, so I could grab a seat and print my stuff before class began. I had two flash drives that I saved my work on, so I had brought both of them with me, just in case one of them decided to stop working for whatever reason and I didn't have time for any shenanigans.

Once I put my flash drive into the computer, I had to wait about a couple of minutes in order for the computer to read it, because all of the computers were running slow at the time. I finally was able to put my information in and proceed with printing my work out, but ran across another problem with so many people trying to print at one time that I had to wait an extra ten minutes for the copy machines to warm back up for it to print because there were too many people at one trying to print their work out. One problem led straight to another, and I stayed another extra twenty minutes, waiting for the student in charge of the library at the time to go get paper so that the rest of us could continue with printing our work out.

I looked at my phone and saw that I had a quarter till class started, so I quickly had to print out my work before anyone else started trying to print something out and headed to class because I didn't know who she wanted to go first. By the time, I walked into class, I saw a group of four people who was placed with the same internship, so they had each other to lean on when it came time to present.

We anxiously waited for her to walk into the classroom so we could go ahead and present and get it over with because the suspense was killing me at that point. As she stepped into the classroom, she told the group that was already standing at the front of the class to go ahead and start and that she was coming right back while she walked right back out of the classroom.

We knew it had to be something going on because she would normally be ready when it's time to present in order to see how we

Life's Scars and Wisdom

were performing and how much we've learned at being future social workers so far.

By the time she came back to the classroom, the first group was already halfway through their presentations and was just about finished, but she didn't hesitate coming in to grill them just a little bit in order to see what they knew since she wasn't present through the whole presentation.

Once one group sat down, the next group got up, ready to present their PowerPoint and get it over with. It's like nothing, but groups were going the first week of presentations, and everyone that had to present by themselves, including me, had to present the second week coming up right along with some other groups. I was kind of bombed that I didn't get to go at first but relieved as well because it gave me a little more time to go back and fix my stuff up a little bit more in order to make it look worth something I put my time into.

The next week, I was determined to present because I got tired of wasting all my good clothes and not being able to present; plus, the suspense and anxiety was kept eating at me, so I hopped out my seat before class ended and headed to the front. I was feeling a little nervous but yet determined that I was going to do great because I knew I worked my ass off on the presentation. My professor had this look on her face with this smirk that always made everybody nervous when going up to present in front of her. As I stood in front of the class, presenting, she asked me why was I looking up and that I needed to be looking at the class. After presenting, she asked me a simple question, which I'm glad she did because she already knew how I was when it came time to present.

As the semester went by, I grew very tired of field on a day-to-day basis, but my field instructor made it worth my while, and we'd have our share of talks and laughs on days I came in kind of weary. My last month there had finally come, and I was steady counting down the days until I was a free man again because it almost felt like I was in jail throughout those months. Our last presentations were coming up that we had to do. We had to create a social step-by-step process on how to treat the client with us being the social worker. This presentation was more important than the other one we had because it actually showed that if what they taught us all these semesters in class actually paid off.

With me feeling the way that I did, my guilt started to kick in right behind it because I knew I paid attention in class sometimes, but not the majority which was why my field placement didn't go as well as it should had. As I cautiously prepared myself for that one, I had to watch a couple YouTube videos to get the feel of what I needed to do, so I proceeded with my slide show, putting everything I did learn and what the videos did together while going by the syllabus at the same time. I had everything labeled out the way that it should've been and got my friend, who helped me the last time, to look over it for me, just so she can see if I had everything put into the right place. I'm glad that she was there to help me with that, right along with my instructor and cousin because they kept me grounded in the real world, especially during my internship, because there were times I felt as if I should've just given up right then and there.

Our final presentations had come, and this time, she was going by alphabetical order on who was going to present based off of our last name, and it was not just anyone going up in front of the class whenever they felt the need to present. There were eight people presenting that first week, eight people presenting the second week, and so on. This one girl in my class and I had the same last name, so she stopped directly with me for presentations that first week. I didn't want to do it, but I was relieved because I had gotten it out the way and didn't have to worry about nothing else but my paperwork from then on.

Time quickly pressed on, and the end of our internship was finally near. With me being overwhelmed that I was actually graduating, I took the last of my paperwork into her office where everyone else was standing around, talking and turning their paperwork in as well. We told our professor we couldn't believe we made it, and her response was "Yeah, y'all made it. Barely but you made it!" That was always her way of joking with us, but then again, it probably wasn't because you never knew how she was coming when it came to our work.

Graduation day had finally came, and I couldn't believe my cousin and I had surpassed this milestone in our life that we worked so hard for, despite the fact of what everyone else said. It was this bittersweet moment because, throughout everything that we've been through, she has always had my back, right or wrong, which is why we're so close to this day. There were some days we'd cry on each other's shoulders while going through this journey because, at one point, we didn't know if we were going to finish with all the classes that we had to drop or didn't come to, because we didn't care about going on certain days, which were a lot!

The valedictorian got up to speak to our graduating class, and she damn near talked for about forty minutes during her speech, which almost put everyone to sleep. As we stood and listened to them to call our names, I couldn't believe that moment in history was actually happening. This experience only made me so much stronger and resilient when it came to being in difficult situations and not knowing the outcome.

As I walked across that stage and grabbed my degree from the president, I knew I had made Mama proud because all she ever wanted from me was to finish school, and that was good enough for her.

I closed that chapter in my life, and now I'm headed to bigger things that awaits me. I really don't know what's in store for me at the moment, but whatever it is, I plan on being great while doing it.

www.ingramcontent.com/pod-product-compliance
Lightning Source LLC
LaVergne TN
LVHW040154080526
838202LV00042B/3162